THE
RICH
MINIMALIST

The Rich Minimalist: An Invitation to Embrace Luxury Living with Less

Byron Tully

Acorn Street Press

Publishing and Design Services: MelindaMartin.me

ISBN: 978-1-950118-21-2 (paperback), 978-1-950118-20-5 (ebook), 978-1-950118-18-2 (hardcover)

THE
RICH
MINIMALIST

AN INVITATION TO

Embrace Luxury Living

WITH LESS

BYRON TULLY

ACORN STREET PRESS

Contents

INTRODUCTION

THIS IS A BOOK ABOUT MINIMALISM. Therefore, a concise introduction is appropriate. The purpose of this book is to show you how to live with fewer material possessions, deliberately, efficiently, and sustainably.

You will live a richer life—and become richer financially—as you implement these strategies and techniques. You will learn to live luxuriously with less, and to embrace the mantra of The Rich Minimalist:

Only the best in my space. Only the best in my life.

Everything else in your life—the excess, the mediocre, the toxic—will be discarded, rejected, replaced, or ignored—or at least kept at a distance and managed effectively.

You may ask, 'Why is the word 'Rich' in the title of this book?' Why do I emphasize money? Because the reality is this: it's very, very difficult to focus on anything else if you're struggling to make ends meet every month.

Yes, the information contained in this book will improve the quality of your life. You'll be delighted to experience this. But don't be surprised when this holistic, 360-degree approach affects your bottom line—your monthly budget, your cash flow, your net worth—almost immediately. This improvement in your finances will give you room to breathe. Room to relax. Room to imagine. Room to grow.

That's the premise of *The Rich Minimalist*: to get your house in order—literally and figuratively—and prosper. Let the journey begin . . .

—Byron Tully
March, 2026
Paris, France

A Brief History of Material Possessions

The best book is not one that imagines a great tale of fiction, nor one that recounts the magnificent history of a country. The best book inspires a story not completely written: the next chapter of your life.

Before we take steps to adopt the Rich Minimalist philosophy in our personal space and daily life, it is important to first change the way we look at 'things.' In order to gain this new perspective on material possessions—and prepare to distance ourselves from them—it will be helpful to review a little history, specifically the history of humans and our relationship with stuff. So let's roll the clock back a few thousand years . . .

We know that prehistoric humans lived in tribes. They collected, fashioned, and used material possessions to construct shelter, create clothing, and hunt for food. Material possessions were primarily tools. By definition, these tools were utilitarian: they had a purpose. That purpose was to help everyone in the tribe survive.

After these material possessions had been collected, fashioned, and used for utilitarian purposes, it probably wasn't long before the chief of the tribe tied a feather onto his spear, just so everyone would know he was the chief. Perhaps he returned from a hunt with an extra animal fur, just to show his wife how much he loved her. It's likely that she then proudly strutted around the cave, showing the other neanderthal ladies what the Big Man on Campus had given her.

At this moment, the role of material possessions in our lives began to expand, to do more than just protect us from the elements, kill prey, and start fires. We instinctively began to communicate with material possessions. We gave material possessions meaning and importance. We gave them weight and power beyond their utility, beyond the value of the elements from which they are made.

At this moment, our problems with material possessions began. This will be discussed in more detail later, but understand it now. This meaning and importance creates attachment. This attachment can cause us problems if we are not aware of it, if we do not take steps to manage it.

Long History, Same Problem

Our misguided relationship with material possessions continued. Historical examples abound.

The pharaohs of Egypt assembled loads of stuff—including furniture, food, combs, and jewelry—to accompany them on their journey into the afterlife. Their tombs could be considered the world's first 'personal storage units'. These wise and worldly rulers were certain these items would be essential in the great beyond. The maxim, "You can't take it with you," never crossed their minds. Nevertheless, the old saying proved true: the dead pharaohs took nothing with them. Their treasures were unearthed by archeologists centuries later and are now on display in museums.

In Renaissance Italy, the height of a Florentine family's residential tower was an expression of their wealth and power. Men spent fortunes just to make sure they had a taller tower than the upstart merchant next door, while their wives probably just rolled their eyes at the whole fiasco. Today, the height of these towers is a historical curiosity at best. It means nothing. Tourists and locals walk past these buildings, oblivious.

In 1626, Native Americans were said to have sold the island of Manhattan to Dutch settlers for $4 and a handful of beads and trinkets. Perhaps this tale is historically accurate. Perhaps not. Still, the gist of the transaction remains: somebody walked away with a few worthless material things that only had emotional value, and somebody walked away with something of real value. Like, you know, an island.

Speaking of the Dutch, in 17th century Holland, tulips became all the rage, eventually being traded on the country's stock exchange. A single bulb—yes, a flower—could cost a fortune. For awhile, prices increased every hour of every day. However, when the market and mania for tulips finally crashed, the country's entire economy followed suit. A lot of people lost a lot of money . . . because they just had to have tulips.

In 18th century France, wigs were popular among men. Not just aristocrats. Almost everybody wore a wig. Wigmakers became rich. We're not talking orthodontist rich. We're talking Silicon Valley rich. A few years later, wigs were no longer in fashion. Wigmakers had made their fortunes. The wigs were discarded. Men went about their business, as many do today, bareheaded.

Present-day examples of foolhardy behavior abound. In Paris, I pass a retail store. I see poor and working class young men lined up to purchase overpriced athletic shoes with a certain logo. I am certain that most of these young men cannot afford these sneakers. Still, they buy them, enriching major corporations and billionaire athletes.

Again, it is the wigmakers who profit.

Lesson: the value of material possessions is in constant flux, usually decreasing over time. This value depends upon the historical and cultural context in which a particular item exists. With the exception of gold bullion, select pieces fine art, and well-chosen real estate, most material things have no real, lasting value. We only think they do.

If we are to effectively adopt Minimalism as a way of life and become wealthy, we must learn to differentiate between something that is actually valuable, essential, or important—an investment or a tool—and something that is a passing fad or something we 'must have' that moment. This requires constant vigilance.

SUMMARY

In order to become comfortable with the idea of 'letting go' of material possessions, we should place them in a historical context. If we place ourselves—and the material possessions we value—in a historical context, we may be able to see 'things' as less valuable than we initially thought, less important to us than we once imagined. This perspective can make it easier to let go of them, live without them, and avoid acquiring more of them in the future.

Exercise: Ask your parents or grandparents about the various stereo systems they purchased during their lifetime. Listen to them describe the size of the speakers and the 'latest' technology that was marketed to them.

Ask about the 'quadraphonic' sound system, which was allegedly going to make 'stereo' systems obsolete in the mid 1970's. Ask them how many different stereo systems (or televisions, or radios) they purchased and where these electronic devices are now.

You can also ask them about ice tea makers, bread makers, crock pots, food processors, fondue pots, lava lamps, the Pet Rock, Beanie Babies, Cabbage Patch Kids, American Dolls, Hummel figurines, and anything from the Franklin Mint.

Listen, and gain historical perspective.

The Meaning of Material Possessions

I am giving you information . . . which will spark contemplation . . . which will alter perspective . . . which will distance you from material possessions . . . which will make it easier to let go . . . which will give you space to really live.

As a young man in college, I took an art history class. In the professor's opening statement to students, he presented this idea: once we have met our basic needs in life— food, clothing, and shelter—everything else we do after that is art. The statement posits that after having met our basic needs, we instinctively begin to express ourselves—in the way we dress, in the way we decorate our homes, in the cars we drive, in so many aspects of our lives.

We can debate the merits of this concept some other time. The important issue we need to address now is how we express ourselves with material possessions. This targets the core of what certain 'things' mean to us.

When we learn what a particular material possession means to us, we can separate our emotion—the memory, the status, the sense of belonging—from the thing itself. Then we can address the psychological issue or feeling in isolation, apart from the material thing. Then we can make more enlightened decisions about the material thing. Maybe we decide not to buy it, to save our money instead, and become wealthier in the process.

For example: when a person says, "I want a Mercedes Benz," what do they really mean? They could mean a number of things:

"I want a Mercedes Benz because it represents a certain lifestyle and communicates that I belong to a certain socioeconomic class."

"I want a Mercedes Benz because I drove a beater for years, and now that I've made it, I want to let my family, friends, and neighbors know I've made it."

"I want a Mercedes Benz because rich people drive Mercedes Benz, and I want everybody to think I'm rich."

"I want a Merceds Benz because I want everybody to respect me."

"I want a Mercedes Benz because it's a safe car to drive, makes sense for my family, and has good resale value."

All of these motivations for wanting a Mercedes Benz are emotionally valid. Everybody wants to 'belong'. Everybody wants to feel proud. Everybody wants to be thought of as successful. Everybody wants respect. To be clear, I'm not bashing anyone for wanting success and the rewards that come with it. I simply want to make you aware of why you want certain things.

Tagore, the great Indian poet and philosopher, once said that we should be suspicious of the things we want. Good advice. I would elaborate by saying that we should constantly be aware of our desire for material things. We should not deny our desires. We are human. We like nice stuff. *Hell, I like nice stuff.*

Acknowledging this, we should investigate the origins of our desires, learn why certain things are important to us, and manage them—the desires and the things—productively. Again, this awareness will help us make fewer, smarter purchases, leaving us with more cash in hand.

Remember: beyond life's bare necessities and tools, material things often represent our emotional needs, needs that we project onto a car, a wristwatch, or a designer handbag, thinking it will satisfy that emotional need or insecurity.

NICHE IDENTITY

Material possessions help us define and communicate our values, passions, interests, and beliefs. When other people share these with us, we often consider them to be members of the our 'tribe.' This tribe can be as broad as membership in a pop singer's fan club or as narrow as the five or six classmates from school with whom you're still very dear friends. Your family may be your most important, enduring tribe.

Often, a tribe or a culture (think hip hop culture, corporate culture, or old money culture) will have distinct modes of dress, certain unspoken rules of behavior, unique traditions and rituals, and common material things of symbolic importance to all members.

For example, everybody understands what is being communicated when an athlete or entertainer from humble means wears a gold Rolex. They've achieved success. They've made it. Good for them. It may be a predictable choice, but in this context a gold Rolex is accepted and even admired by their friends, family, and fans.

However, when a tech bro hits it big, he probably won't buy a gold Rolex. He'll probably just buy a new hoodie and fly private from now on. Who knows? What we do know is that he doesn't live and work in a flashy culture. He's a member of a different tribe. He makes different choices.

Each individual's background, tribe, culture, and aspirations dictate the meaning and importance that material possessions have for them. These also dictate which material possessions they'll acquire, when they'll acquire them, and how much they'll acquire.

Examine your own background, tribe, culture, and aspirations. Consider the common material possessions that your family or peers desire, acquire, and display. How closely do you follow these purchasing patterns? Do your possessions serve you well? Or are these choices just bad consumer habits that slow your progress to financial independence and wealth?

While being a member of a tribe and having a niche identity is important, we should carefully examine the expectations that go along with that identity, especially with regards to material possessions. You can still belong to your tribe. You can still embrace your identity. You can still honor your traditions. However, you aren't obligated to purchase all the things that other members of your tribe purchase.

Note: when you identify on a personal level with a name brand of clothing or any other consumer product, you have succumbed to an illusion. The illusion is that owning a name brand handbag, wristwatch, car, or pair of sneakers makes you a part of a group, gives you status in a community, or increases your value as a person.

The reality is much harsher: major corporations manufacture millions of 'exclusive' products every year. They use advertising and influencers to convince you that, if you buy this product, you will be this person. You will have things in common with this or that celebrity.

None of these things are true. What is true is that you will likely have traded your hard-earned money for their well-marketed product, and there will be very little positive change in your life after the transaction. Only a negative change in your bank account. Your identity must be independent of labels and logos.

Remember: your best tribe is one that prioritizes constructive values and encourages excellence in life and work. The members of your tribe should engage with you from a place of love. They should support you, be honest with you, and not pressure you to buy or do things that don't line up with your goals.

THE ARISTOS

During my time here in France, I've lived in Paris and in the French countryside. I've met a variety of people. School teachers, boutique owners, farmers, politicians, artists, and aristocrats.

For our purposes, the aristocrats may be the most interesting and helpful to examine. Some are very rich. Others are of modest means. Some dress well. Some barely give their clothing a thought.

They are well-mannered, of course. Educated, without a doubt. Intelligent, for the most part. Keenly aware of their surroundings. (I refer to both the cafes in which we met and the world in which we live.) Most importantly, they possess a rock-hard, unshakeable sense of who they are. Their identity is definite and deep-seated on a molecular level. They are aristocrats, with centuries of family history, breeding, education, and experience. Their outlook is unique. Their attitudes, sometimes peculiar. Their certainty about themselves, unassailable.

Whether they are grandly holding forth in a chateau or barely holding on in a studio apartment, it matters not: they are who they are. The environment in which they were raised, the manner in which they were educated, the obligations they inherited, the privileges they enjoyed—all these factors—not material things—forged them into the people they are.

These aristocrats offer us an example . . . and an opportunity. The example is to know that regardless of what life throws at us (and many of these people and their families have seen some dramatic ups and downs) we must define and hold fast to our own individual identity based on ourselves—our values, our priorities, our accomplishments—not our material possessions.

We must be independent of circumstances, aloof to hardship, and nonchalant toward material things that can be confiscated, destroyed, lost, or stolen. Only then can we define ourselves. Only then can we know where our true strength originates. Only then can we appreciate where our real treasure resides. This awareness gives us enduring power, even as material possessions inevitably come and go throughout our lives.

Fear, Phobia, and Insecurity

Often, we become overly attached to and accumulate an excess of material things because of fear, phobia, or insecurity. If we really split hairs, perhaps fear and insecurity are the same or similar, but I'll address them separately.

Fear is being worried about what will happen if we don't have a certain possession. If we don't have a car, how will we survive? If we don't have a television, how will life go on? If we aren't on social media, how can we possibly function in society? Okay, social media isn't a material thing, but it is an issue, which we'll address later. Fear often visits us when we underestimate our ability to be flexible and resourceful. It also is a result of facing the unknown and the unfamiliar. "I'm afraid of what might happen," is a common sentiment.

We may fear what will happen if we let go of a particular material possession. For example, we may worry that we'll forget our grandfather if we don't hold onto his old, non-working pocket watch that sits in a box in the closet that we only look inside of once or twice a year. The truth is this: the memories of your grandfather will be with you forever. All you have to do is mark his birthday on a calendar. When that day comes, take a moment, quietly acknowledge your time together and the fond memories, and then go on. You don't need a 'thing' to do that.

What options do I have? What's the worst that can happen? What's the best that can happen? What actions can I take? What are the possible consequences or possible rewards? These questions are tools to use in order to move through life, to acknowledge fear, cut it down to size, and conquer it. To cure worry through work.

Phobia is the business of mental health professionals. This is a situation in which a person is suffering from an extreme belief that has no basis in logic or reality. I can't help anyone who has a phobia about what they need to hold onto and what things mean to them. Hoarders who have every square inch of their residence piled to the ceiling with stuff? That's emotional territory that I am unqualified to address. If that's you, please get professional help. I wish you the best.

Most of the time, it is only insecurity that confronts us when we face the prospect of letting go of things and living with less. This is because most of our waking lives are governed by habit and reinforced by social conditioning. We are creatures of habit and loyal followers of the familiar. We succumb to peer pressure. We opt for convenience. We are influenced by advertising. Surrounded by a multitude of products that are constantly on offer and easily available, we often find it easier to buy something than to think about something or to do something.

However, we can adjust and improve our lives quite easily. How? By replacing one habit with another.

For example, a friend of mine had a problem with online shopping. One day, she decided to ride her stationary bike every time she felt the urge to look for a new purse. In two months, she was in very good shape, physically, emotionally, and financially. She still enjoys her purses, but she enjoys good health more. She simply chose to alter her behavior, to replace one habit with another. "Instead of doing this, I'm going to do this . . . " Don't try to 'break' a bad habit. Just replace it with a good one.

Another source of insecurity is the feeling that we won't be disciplined enough to successfully, permanently change our behavior. Don't worry. If you follow the steps I outline here, you will gain a better understanding of your relationship with things. You will then be able to discard material things more easily. Subsequently, you will discover the space—physical and emotional—to invite more joyful experiences to come into your life. It's less about discipline and more about strategy.

Know this: if I repeat myself in this book, it's not because I forgot what I've written. I repeat myself because I want you to remember what I've written.

Summary

Material possessions have meaning to us.

When we acknowledge this reality, we can manage their negative impact on us. We manage the impact by understanding the connection of material possessions to our identity, how much of 'who we are' is 'what we own'.

Our identity is not only our name, age, gender, marital status, or occupation. It also encompasses our background, our culture, our tribe, our aspirations, and our insecurities.

We must separate material possessions from our identity.

Exercise: Visit a local cafe where a variety of people come and go. Train stations and shopping malls work well, too. Pull up a chair in the corner. Order a coffee. Pretend to look at your phone or, better yet, a newspaper. Now, discreetly watch people come and go.

Note their choice of clothing, especially their accessories. Note the designer sunglasses. Note the branded handbag. Note the expensive watch. Note the logos and the labels. Note the obvious. What do they tell you about the people wearing them. What do these people want to communicate? Are you impressed? Are you envious?

There are no right or wrong answers, just revelations.

How to Look at Material Possessions

Material possessions often represent the tangible rewards of our labor, the manifestation of our dreams, the harvest of our toil. However, they are not the most valuable of things.

Our true treasure is the strength found in purpose, the courage found in challenge, the joy found in learning, the satisfaction found in accomplishment.

As I've noted, our problems with material possessions frequently originate in the meaning and importance we attach to them, beyond the utility and convenience they provide. Emotion tied to symbolism and status. That's what we're dealing with. What a 'thing' symbolizes to us personally, and the status it conveys (in our minds, anyway) to other people.

To help us dismantle these usually unhelpful concepts, let's look at the material possession from a different point of view. We're going to shift our perspective as the purchaser or consumer of the desired product and position ourselves as someone who is selling or servicing the product.

Let's say you're considering the purchase of a diamond bracelet. After seeing it online or in magazine ads, you've convinced yourself that you must have it. It's sparkly and beautiful. It would look so good on your wrist. You deserve it!

Before you buy it, though, shift your perspective. Place yourself on the other side of the jewelry store counter. You're now the salesperson. (Don't get too comfortable: in a moment you'll be the owner of the store, and then a vice president of sales at the company that manufactures the diamond bracelet.)

As the salesperson, you want somebody to buy this damn bracelet. You'll get a commission on the sale. You don't care about how it impacts their financial situation.

You don't care if, a year later, this same customer is taking the bracelet to a pawn shop to see what they can get for it because they've lost their job and the rent is due. That's their problem.

Next, you're the owner of the jewelry store. You have overhead to cover, rent on the retail space, employee salaries, a mortgage, a lazy kid in college. You've got nine or ten lines of diamond bracelets, necklaces, rings, earrings . . . you name it. If it's gold, silver, platinum, or just shiny, you've got it and you need to sell it. Today, tomorrow, next week, next month, every day. It's product. It's inventory. It's cash flow. It's business. You, too, need to sell that damn bracelet.

Finally, as the vice president of sales for the company that manufactures the bracelet, you must monitor trends, design new products, schmooze with your retailers, size up the competition, consider lab-grown diamonds (!), and make sure you hit your sales target so you can get your year-end bonus.

Now that you've put yourself in the position of these people who make and sell diamond bracelets for a living every day like so many hamburgers on a grill, pause for a moment. Look again at this sparkling trinket that you are certain means so much to you. Do you think they share your perspective? Do they feel the emotion, the symbolism, the status that this bracelet promises? They don't. They simply want to sell something and make a profit. There's nothing wrong with that. For them, it's all business. What is it for you? All emotion?

When you enter a transaction emotionally and the other party enters it objectively, your chances of making a bad deal increase.

(Quick aside: ask your older relatives about the diamond 'tennis bracelet' that was all the rage a few decades ago.)

As a second example, consider your local automobile mechanic. Every day, he changes an oil filter, replaces a transmission, listens for a valve going bad, or fixes a flat tire. Every day, he sees Toyotas, BMW's, Volvos, Range Rovers, Hondas, and yes, our previously-mentioned Mercedes Benz. Does he have a passion for cars? He might. He might have a real love for vintage Volkswagens.

Still, he sees cars for what they are: an assembly of steel frames and rubber tires, nuts and bolts, hoses and clamps, plastic and wood, glass and chrome. That's what cars are to him: modes of transportation that need constant maintenance and repair. Some are efficient and a good value for the money. Some are poorly made, expensive to service, and in need of constant repair. Some are a good deal for the owner. Some are, let's face it, a good deal for him.

Do you think he's impressed when the owner of a luxury car pulls up in his parking lot in need of his expertise? Probably not. He's considering which service they'll need and how much he'll charge for it. Again, it's business.

Again, now that you've seen a diamond bracelet from the jeweler's perspective and an automobile from the mechanic's perspective, you have the opportunity to take the emotion, the symbolism, and the status out of material possessions. See them from a different perspective. You'll do this because it's all business for you, too. Only your business is to be happier, to live a richer life, and hold onto more of your money.

Note: material things can make you happy. For awhile. It is best if we understand the limits of this happiness.

With a little reflection, we can more accurately assess the role we want material things to play in our lives. When we view ourselves and material things in a different context—when we see them for what they really are—it is often easier to manage our desire for them or live without them entirely.

Material possessions are not relationships. They are not accomplishments. They may symbolize these or be a result of these, but they are not these.

SUMMARY

In order to disconnect and distance ourselves from material possessions, we can look at them the way vendors look at them: as products that must be sold, repaired, and maintained.

From this perspective, material possessions can be seen for what they are: products that we use and benefit from, apart from what they mean to us emotionally.

We can also deconstruct material possessions, mentally breaking down the individual components from which they're made, or identifying the materials used to create them.

Exercise: Identify a material possession that has tremendous meaning for you. It can be one that you already own, or one that you aspire to own.

Let's say it is a Hermes leather belt. Lots of status. Quality craftsmanship, no doubt. Impressive, especially with a pair of faded jeans, simple white shirt or blouse, and some quality loafers. *Tres chic.*

Now, itemize the materials that actually make up the belt. There is leather, of course, and the metal that the buckle is made from. Anything else? Leather and metal. That's it. For a very serious retail price.

Now, select the material possession that is Your Personal Kryptonite: the shoes, the handbag, the watch. The thing you value too much and cannot resist. What is it composed of? Make a list of the leather, the metal, the glass—whatever—and acknowledge that the materials you listed are what this material possession really is.

The thing is not the emotion you associate with it. It's a thing.

The First Step to De-Clutter

To be victorious, retreat.

Everything that you've read in this book so far has been presented intentionally. Mine is a gentle approach, a subtle strategy. I have encouraged you to consider material possessions in a historical context. To contemplate the meaning that material possessions have in your life, to assess your material possessions from different points of view, with a more detached attitude.

This gradual, nuanced process makes it easier to let go of material things and, as a result, live a richer life. Our next small step is to identify the categories in which our material possessions fall. We will also take our First Action: de-cluttering a small part of our living space.

First, categories! Here we go . . .

Essential: some of our material possessions are absolutely essential. These include shelter (where we live) and clothing (what we wear). I don't consider food a material possession, as it comes and goes. Being attached or addicted to food is a problem for some people, but it's not an issue I'm qualified to address. So we'll just focus on our residence and and our clothing as essential.

Utilitarian: some of our material possessions are very useful. Our lives would be unreasonably inconvenient without them, and we may suffer if we don't own them and use them. These include pots and pans, plates and silverware, furniture, toothbrushes and combs. If we live in a rural area, a car may be utilitarian and almost essential. The important distinction here is to know what is truly essential and/or utilitarian, and what is simply nice to have, which is our next category.

Creature comforts: these are things that are, as I say, nice to have. A television is nice to have, but it's not essential. If you live in a metropolitan area, a car is nice to have, but it may not be essential. It is not essential that you have five winter coats. 'Collectors editions' of ceramic figurines or sports memorabilia are not essential or utilitarian. You see where I'm going with this.

Luxuries: Luxuries are things that you enjoy that are not only creature comforts—they are the best of creature comforts, and often the most expensive of creature comforts. They are never essential and may or may not have utilitarian value. Other options could suffice just as well. A wool coat may keep you warm just as well as a fur coat. A Timex watch tells time just as well as a Cartier watch. A luxury item is purchased for its aesthetic value, its design, its craftsmanship, its materials, perhaps its function, but most importantly for the way it makes you feel when you see it, wear it, or use it. Emotional satisfaction weighs heavily in the luxury category.

It may surprise you to know that I value luxury highly. I enjoy it regularly. It is an important part of The Rich Minimalist life. However, in order to embrace it fully and appreciate it appropriately, we must get rid of the junk—material and emotional—first. So, first things first.

We need to categorize everything we own as Essential, Utilitarian, a Creature Comfort, or a Luxury. This can be a relatively easy thing to do. We look at a drinking glass and decide that it's pretty utilitarian. When we're thirsty, we drink water or juice out of a glass. Much easier than slurping out of the faucet or guzzling out of the bottle. However, what if we have 35 drinking glasses?

Quantity is our first filter when we look at embracing The Rich Minimalist philosophy. After we determine that an item is essential or utilitarian, how many of that thing do we need?

Quality will be our second filter later on in this process. But right now, we must thin the herd.

Let's start in your bedroom with a straightforward task.

The Easy De-Clutter

This is your First Action. Your first step toward becoming a Rich Minimalist. It's fairly predictable. Quite accessible. Very simple. Maybe not so easy.

Walk into your bedroom and look around. Bed, pillows, sheets, lamp, nightstand, chair, chest of drawers, mirror. Pretty essential. So far, so good. Now, step to your closet. Open the door. Look inside. Here are your clothes. Quite essential, they protect us from the elements and prevent us from being charged with indecent exposure. More importantly, they provide us with the appropriate attire for work and comfortable outfits for weekends.

Our wardrobe is also a primary mode of expression: we often communicate to others our tastes, ambitions, tribe, status, social class, and wealth by the clothes we wear. All of those attempts to communicate—successfully and unsuccessfully— reside in our closets. What also resides here is an emotional chronology in the form of garments: our past moments of elation, depression, compulsive purchasing, and 'under the influence of influencers' fashion mistakes.

We shopped when we came into some money, when we got a new job, when we broke up with a lover, when we were bored, when we felt insecure and just had to have that new thing that would make us feel like we belonged.

It's all here. A line up of The Usual Suspects. Some with the price tags still attached. Buried emotions and unused items are two things we address harshly in The Rich Minimalist culture. Time to purge.

First, let's attack the items you haven't worn in a year. (Not seasonal items you'll wear when the weather changes in a few months.) These garments are never going to be worn again, but they are still on clothes hangers and shelves in your closet. "But I worked hard for the money that paid for that!" you might say when confronted with the idea of getting rid of a garment. Yeah, exactly. Think about that next time you make an emotional purchase.

Shoes, blouses, shirts, skirts, jackets, pants, suits, sweaters, socks, coats. Everything is up for review . . . .and disposal. Throw all of your clothes on the bed and start sorting ruthlessly.

The success of this process, like many things in life, is going to depend upon how honest you are with yourself. So, be a merciless, pillaging pirate. Growl as you throw things in a bag for charity. Grrrrr!!!

Seriously, as you proceed, as yourself a few questions. Question: does the article of clothing represent an emotional need or a physical need? For the most part, your clothes should address physical needs. The two big physical factors are usually work and weather: what we need to wear to the office and what we need to wear to keep warm. Emotional needs are fulfilled by your vocation, your friends, and your family. Identify and separate the physical needs from the emotional needs.

Question: what are you wearing every day? Those items will survive the first cut and be spared. For now. What do you need to wear to work?

Reality Check: you can wear a few things over and over again and mix it up with some accessories. Sad Reality Check: unless you work at Vogue magazine, no one in your office is really keeping tabs on your fashion choices.

Later, we'll talk about The Uniform and how that concept can make your life easier and save you money. But for now, let's address the waste. This is Phase One. Getting rid of things that are obviously not being used. Start in your closet. Then go to your drawers. Closet by closet, drawer by drawer.

Critically review the mistakes made that involve BOGO (Buy One, Get One free!) and FOMO (Fear Of Missing Out, i.e., Sale ends Saturday!) advertising strategies. Again, remember: that pile of unused and unwanted garments sitting there is your money, not used to its best and highest purpose. Toss the unused and obsolete into a box. Take that box to the charity shop. Donate it.

THE FILTER PROCESS

We all know what a filter is. It is a mechanism that allows some things to pass through and other things to be restrained. For our purposes, the Filter Process for your clothing is a list of questions:

- What am I wearing every day?

- How many of these everyday items do I really need?

- Which ones are the best, i.e., in the best condition, of the best quality, and the most functional?

This process is often slow and uneven. If you change your mind a few times about a few items, that's normal. Don't sweat it. Just make progress.

In terms of the clothes in your closet, try to reduce your inventory to the following:

- 6 shirts or blouses
- 6 pairs of pants (jeans, chinos, or slacks)
- 3 skirts or dresses
- 3 jackets
- 3 sweaters
- 2 coats
- 5 pairs of shoes (if you're a guy) and
- 10 pairs of shoes (if you're a gal).

You need enough garments to rotate between wearing and washing. Otherwise, if you only have two pair of pants, let's say, they will get worn and washed too often and wear out prematurely. That costs you money and defeats the purpose of being a Rich Minimalist.

You will also consider versatility as you reduce your clothing inventory. An item that can be worn at work and on the weekends has added value. So prioritize it. Items that are strictly formal or otherwise 'occasion specific' have less value. A simple black dress, for example, can be worn for work, weekend events, and formal events. A black men's suit or blue blazer can be worn for work, weekend events, and formal events.

Again, reduce quantity, prioritize quality, and weigh versatility. Emotions will challenge you during this process. Oh, but that's so cute! Oh, but this has so many memories for me! Oh,

I wore this on our first date! When these emotions arise, you will need to take a moment.

Go through the following step-by-step process:

- Honor the memory attached to this garment.

- Be grateful for that memory.

- Remember the feeling you associate with the garment.

- Accept that what you feel for the garment is really what you feel for the memory—the event, the moment, the person—what this garment symbolizes.

Again, what it symbolizes is not what it is. It's a jacket. It's a shirt. It's a dress. It's a coat. Wool, cotton, linen, silk. Buttons, stitching, zippers. Color, pattern, texture. That's what it is. It will eventually fade, fray, tear, and dissolve, but your memory of what it represents is eternal. Define its meaning and hold onto that. Let the garment go. It can benefit someone else, create more memories for them, and free you to move on.

If you want more and better in your life—and in your closet—you'll need to make room for it. This is part of the process. Start with your clothes. Take your time, but make sure something goes every weekend for one month. That's four Saturday morning reviews of your wardrobe. Four opportunities to filter, offering you time to consider and decide. Four trips to the charity shop.

This one-month schedule for your First Action is optimal. Do it all at once, and you risk throwing away things you actually need and use. Do it over a three month period, and you never get rid of all the waste.

SUMMARY

We must mentally categorize material possessions as Essential, Utilitarian, a Creature Comfort, or a Luxury. As we categorize items, we can more easily determine if we really need them or if we can live without them.

After we categorize items, we then use filters. These filters are Quantity—how many of a particular item we have, as we consider how many we really need—and Quality, how well-made a particular item is, which will tell us how long we can expect it to last.

By categorizing and filtering, we can reduce the number of material things in our space and increase the quality of material things in our space. This process will enable us to de-clutter with less emotional conflict and to live easily and efficiently with fewer items.

Our First Action is to take an inventory of the clothes in our closet. We discard garments we haven't worn in the past 12 months. We prioritize garments we wear every day. We value the well-made, the versatile, and the classic. We eliminate the trashy, the trendy, and the tired.

Exercise: As you de-clutter your closet, keep a small journal and make note of your feelings and thoughts regarding this process. It may help you address emotions that arise as you categorize, filter, retain, and discard.

Please note: I've structured this book strategically. You will first be encouraged to think, consider, alter your perspective, and only then, after those steps, take action.

You've absorbed a substantial amount of information thus far, and taken one action. Let's consider a Second Action.

The Backpack, the Suitcase, and the Steamer Trunk

Practice, and all things come.

At this point, I'm going to offer you three exercises to help you become comfortable with owning fewer garments. These are The Backpack Approach, The Vacation Suitcase Approach, and the Steamer Trunk Approach.

Obvious in their titles, they will nevertheless require rigor in their execution. I offer options to you because, as with many endeavors, the paths are many, but the goal is one. Therefore, select the approach that works for you. Or try all of them. You'll find what resonates and benefit.

This is your Second Action. Execute it thoughtfully.

The Backpack Approach

If you would like to learn exactly how few garments you need in order to function on a daily or weekly basis, consider the Backpack Approach.

Begin by pulling your trusty backpack out of the closet (do not use this exercise as an excuse to buy a new backpack). If you have a small piece of carry-on luggage, you can use it as well.

Here are the steps to follow for the Backpack Approach: first, get dressed. Wear your most versatile, functional ensemble. It is important to layer garments, as these will be the only garments you can wear that are not included in your backpack.

Consider the following:

- a shirt or blouse

- a sweater

- a jacket—blue blazer or tweed a winter coat, if the weather requires it

- a versatile pair of pants (jeans, chinos, or wool pants)

- a dress or skirt (optional), and

- walkable shoes—maybe sneakers, maybe boots— depending on your professional wardrobe requirements and, again, the weather.

Second, pull out a few pairs of underwear and socks, a few dress shirts or blouses, a pair of pants, a cosmetics or shave kit, and your laptop. These items—the ones you are not wearing—must fit into your backpack.

Imagine you're going on a weekend getaway. Only this getaway is going to last 10 days. You're going to live and work wearing only the items in your backpack. So you will do the old 'wash and wear' rotation of the same items of clothing over a consecutive 10-day period of time.

Therefore, choose your garments wisely. Weigh their versatility, functionality, and comfort for work and leisure alike. If you have shoes or garments exclusively used for working out, you'll have to fit those in to your backpack as well, or figure out a different workout for the 10-day Backpack Approach.

This approach, and the two that follow, offer valuable benefits:

- They help you recognize and appreciate your most functional, versatile, and easy-to-care-for items, the real superstars of your daily wardrobe.

- They help you learn to mix and match effectively with a limited rotation of garments. (Hint: consider easy-to-pack scarves for style and variety.)

- They help you shatter the illusion that you need a lot of clothes in order to function on a daily basis.

- They help you develop an instinct for which garments work best for you as you curate a more refined, Rich Minimalist wardrobe going forward.

Now, close your closet door, and live out of your backpack for 10 days. Good luck. At the end of 10 days, reflect on the experience. Which garments worked best? Which were useless? Which ones do you really need?

The Suitcase Approach

If you are uncertain about which items of clothing you should discard and which items you should keep, and you want to work with more garments than The Backpack Approach allows, consider the Suitcase Approach.

This approach allows you to pack a larger quantity of garments. However, it requires that you live out of the suitcase for one month, not just the 10 days I prescribed in the Backpack Approach. Ouch.

To start, pull out a large suitcase, a piece of luggage you would use for a two week vacation. You want to pack comfortable, useful, versatile garments for daily wear, but you'll also want to pack a nice garment or two for elegant evenings. And the weather may vary, so consider layering opportunities and being appropriately dressed while active.

Again, choosing garments wisely is important. Versatility is key. Being able to mix, match, and repeat is paramount. A heavy coat, a jacket, a shirt, pants, and one pair of shoes will be worn by you as you depart on your hypothetical journey, so they are not included in the items that go into your suitcase.

Lingerie, scarves, neckties, additional shoes, hair dryer, curling iron, razors, and cosmetics, however, must go into the suitcase. Oh, and don't forget to pack garments that are easy to take care of. You'll have more clothes with you this time, but you'll still be doing the 'wash and wear' thing to a large extent.

Okay. Select garments from your closet and drawers, and pack your single large suitcase. Close your suitcase. Set it against the wall. Look at it. Now, mentally lock your closet and your drawers. Live out of that suitcase for a month. Again, wear only the garments in that suitcase for a month. Wash and wear them as often as you like. No cheating.

After 30 days, assess the experience. Did you go into your closet or drawers for additional items? Did you need to? Or did you just want to? Which garments were not useful? Which garments were most useful?

If you pretty much lived out of your large suitcase for a month without much of an issue, why keep the other clothes in your closet? You don't need them. They are just taking up space. They are just reminding you of who you once were. Not who you are. Not who you will be. Let them go.

This exercise will show you that embracing The Rich Minimalist philosophy is not as difficult as you might imagine. Yes, you may grow bored with the limited rotation of clothes in your suitcase.

However, you may also welcome the convenience and simplicity of just grabbing a shirt and a pair of pants with minimal thought. You'll get dressed quickly. You'll meet your day smoothly, without rummaging through obsolete garments in order to find something that matches something else, that will go with these shoes, that will be right for this event, blah blah blah.

THE STEAMER TRUNK APPROACH

This third and final approach to rethinking and reimagining your wardrobe is similar to the Suitcase Approach, but offers even more garments to choose from, and perhaps a more permanent storage solution for your clothes. It is the Steamer Trunk Approach.

In centuries past, sophisticated travelers often packed their clothing and personal items in a steamer trunk, so named for the steam-powered boats that were often the means of transportation for long voyages. The trunks haven't changed much in design, construction, or materials over the years.

Today, they are often used by young people attending boarding school or summer camp, and underused by adults seeking a functional and versatile piece of luggage/furniture/ storage space.

Substantial at a standard size of 50 inches long, 30 inches wide, and 30 inches tall, the steamer trunk has two basic interior layouts. The first, a vertical interior configuration, includes clothes hangers and interior drawers. The trunk is opened and used 'standing up', as it were.

The second design is horizontal, with the trunk designed to sit flat, and open from the top. When the lid is opened, a shallow, compartmentalized tray presents itself, perfect for personal items. When the tray is removed, a large open storage space presents itself, allowing the owner to stack clothing, books, cigars, and dueling pistols. (Okay, maybe not the pistols.)

The horizontal steamer trunk has added value: it can conveniently store items while the traveler is at home. The steamer trunk can often be found at the foot of the bed, in front of a fireplace, used as a living room coffee table, or nestled discreetly under a window sill.

For our purposes, it provides a wonderful, nostalgic challenge: how much of your clothing and personal items can you fit in a single steamer trunk? Can you live out of your steamer trunk for an extended period of time? Perhaps permanently? Can you muster the discipline, taste, and discretion necessary in order to curate an elegant but restrained wardrobe and a limited but luxurious coterie of personal items, all within the constraints of a single steamer trunk?

I challenge you, monsieur! I challenge you, madame! Acquire a steamer trunk and do your best!

Again, as you address the clothes in your closet, allow this filtering process to proceed over a 4-week period. Use an hour or so each Saturday morning of the month to review, consider, discard, and refine your wardrobe. Go slowly, but make progress. Donate or trash obviously obsolete or excess items immediately. Get. Them. Out. Of. Your. Residence.

Take a moment with other items that you are less certain of. Let the new feeling of space and freedom in your closet slowly sink in. Then think about the Backpack, Suitcase, or Steam Trunk approach.

SUMMARY

You do not need as many clothes as you think you do. In order to become more comfortable with this reality, there are three exercises that you can do, three approaches that you can take.

The first is the Backpack Approach. This involves packing all the clothes you need for a 10-day period of time into a single backpack. All the garments, except the ones you are wearing, fit into the backpack. These items are the only ones you wear during the 10-day period of time.

The second is the Suitcase Approach. This involves packing all the clothes you need for a 30-day period of time into a single suitcase. All the garments, except the ones you are wearing, fit into the suitcase. These items are the only ones you wear during the 30-day period of time.

The third is the Steamer Trunk Approach. This involves packing all the clothes you need for an extended period of time into a single Steamer Trunk. All the garments, except the ones you are wearing, fit into the steamer trunk. These items are the only ones you wear for an extended period of time, or even permanently.

Exercise. Before you embark upon one of these approaches, lay out a few of your favorite garments. Rank them in order of quality, versatility, functionality, and comfort.

Are they well made? Can they work for you in a variety of scenarios? At work? On weekends? For social events? Do they keep you warm? Or just look good? Are they comfortable to wear for extended periods?

This review will serve you well as you decide which garments to select for your particular approach.

The Room-by-Room Approach

We often find beauty in function.

In previous chapters, I've introduced information and concepts to help you develop a more nuanced perspective toward material possessions. I have also introduced exercises to help you streamline your wardrobe. The intent is to change the way you see 'stuff' and to gently familiarize you with the idea of 'living with less'.

Now that you've become comfortable with those concepts and have 'dipped your toe in the water' with the concepts and the clothes, let's go room by room in your residence and address the material possessions within each.

It's easier to go room by room. There's no need to be overwhelmed by trying to clean out and reorganize your entire place in one fell swoop. As we proceed, we're going to first consider the function of each room. As we consider function, we can then identify which material possessions are appropriate for that space.

This is your Third Action.

Again, be thorough, thoughtful, and deliberate. Every item in each room is up for review. Every item that does not follow function is a candidate for removal.

Remember our categories: essential, utilitarian, creature comforts, and luxuries. Also keep in mind our 'quality' and 'quantity' filters. Again, the success of this exercise will be determined by how rigorously you apply the categories and the filters.

Note: I am detailing each room, the bedroom, the bathroom, the kitchen, and the living room. Of course, if you live in a studio apartment, you will need to adjust and apply these principles to a particular 'area', rather than a particular room.

The Bedroom

The bedroom is the place you go to sleep, to dress, to be alone with your thoughts, and to be intimate. Psychologically and emotionally, this is the most important room in your residence. It is also the most personal and private. Therefore, it is very important to keep it clean, organized, and clutter-free. It is also important to furnish it only with items that conform with the function of the bedroom.

The first function is to sleep. Therefore, you will need a bed. Many people are content to buy the cheapest bed on the market. Not The Rich Minimalist. Why? Because you spend one third of your life in bed. You spend much of this time sleeping, giving your body and mind a chance to rest and recharge.

Properly rested, you will be ready to tackle the next day's challenges. If you don't rest well, you won't perform well. You won't be in the best mood. You won't make the best decisions. So your bed, and to a similar extent your pillows and sheets, have a large impact on your life.

Invest wisely in a good bed, even if you have to delay the acquisition of other pieces of furniture. Invest in high-quality bed linens, as well. Watch for sales on both beds and bed linens. Don't be afraid to consider display model beds that may be offered for less money.

Note: your bed should be elevated, high off the ground. Sleeping on a futon or air mattress near the floor can make you feel less than your best.

The second function is to dress. The bedroom is the place where you get dressed and undressed. Therefore, it should have adequate space for your clothes. This space is either a closet or a piece of furniture that contains your garments. This piece of furniture is often a chest of drawers, wardrobe, or steamer trunk. Your bedroom should also have a small chair or stool to sit on as you get dressed or undressed.

The third function is to be alone with your thoughts. A place to sit, put your feet up, and read. A small nightstand will provide a place for a lamp, a book, a clock, your phone, or your eyeglasses. Having this designated place for your personal items allows your mind to rest—for a few minutes or for an entire night—knowing that there's a place for everything, and everything is in its place.

You may decide to have your Spiritual Space in your bedroom. As I mentioned, this is the place for your altar, religious statues or images, or simply a candle. This space is separate from your nightstand, but maybe on a small table of similar size.

The fourth function is to be intimate. The bedroom is frequently the place where you make love with your partner. It is also a place where you can spend special moments reading bedtime stories to your children. Therefore, the colors, fabrics, framed pictures, and wall coverings you choose should contribute to relaxation, to intimacy, to comfort, to warmth, to tenderness, and to love. Choose wisely.

To recap, The Rich Minimalist Bedroom is furnished with the following:

- a bed

- a nightstand or two

- a lamp or two

- a chair or stool

- chest of drawers, a steamer trunk, or an armoire (wardrobe)

- a stationary bicycle, yoga mat, and

- light weights (optional).

For the unfurnished bedroom, it's best to acquire the bed first, then to slowly add the rug, furniture, and lamp. The approach for the furnished bedroom in need of an overhaul is, of course, different. My best advice, as you'll recall, is as follows:

- pull all of your clothes and personal items out of the closet and drawers and pile them on the bed;

- begin the process of categorizing each item as essential, utilitarian, creature comfort, or luxury;

- consider the quality of each item (is it the best? or is it junk?);

- consider the quantity of each item (do I really need 20 t-shirts?);

- filter according to date: the the last time you've used an item (is it more than 12 months?);

- filter according frequency: to how often you use an item (every day? or less than twice a year?).

The high-quality, timeless, and versatile garments that you wear on a regular basis go back into your closet. Essential and utilitarian items will remain on your bed or be put back in their place, whether that's a table, the nightstand, chest of drawers, or the closet. Creature comforts are up for a hard review, as are less-than-stellar luxury items. Everything is on the chopping block.

Question: if you're not using these things regularly, why do you still have them?

Please note: empty cardboard boxes or large plastic trash bags will come in handy, as obsolete or redundant items will go into these containers, to be promptly donated to charity.

Again, this approach works for clothing and for personal items, as you will find both in your bedroom.

Again, we start this process in the bedroom because it is the most personal and intimate space you live in. If the bedroom is in order, we can proceed to the next room. If the bedroom is not in order, nothing else really matters.

Again, we use categories and filters to weed out the excess, erode emotional resistance, and reduce clothing and personal items to only the most essential . . . and only the best.

The watchword for the bedroom is 'sanctuary.'

THE BATHROOM

The bathroom is the second most personal space you inhabit. The bathroom functions as a place where you go to keep yourself clean. Cleanliness is essential to health. So this space is important.

This room usually has little or no furniture and very few clothes. Bath towels, hand towels, and wash clothes can be numerous or few (few is better). A bar of soap, shampoo and conditioner, hairdryer and/or curling iron, toothbrush and toothpaste, floss, combs and brushes, and some incidental over-the-counter or prescription drugs . . . and we've pretty much itemized the material possessions usually found in a bathroom.

So where do we run into problems? Cosmetics. First, let me say this: I know everyone wants to look nice and feel attractive. That's completely understandable. Furthermore, I would never tell anyone which beauty products they need or how many beauty products they need, even if they only use a fraction of those products on a daily basis. (The beauty industry itself estimates that 20 to 40% of its product is purchased, never used, and becomes waste.)

The only thing I would recommend is that each person take an inventory of the cosmetics they currently own. Then, as I've recommended previously, mercilessly filter out the products that are not being used. How many shades of lipstick do you need? How many mascaras, makeup brushes, sponges, foundations, primers, cover sticks, glosses, lip pencils, eye liners, lash curlers, highlighters, eye shadows, blush, and bottles of nail polish are necessary?

As you ask yourself these questions, remember, again, that the excess represents money spent. Money that could have been used to contribute to your financial independence.

Haircare products can also be another 'money vampire', sucking the life out of your financial progress. The cost of braids, extensions, and wigs can be considerable. Think about your choices. Look good, but be smart.

Remember: intelligence is attractive. Purpose is attractive. Kindness is attractive. A sense of humor is attractive. Generosity is attractive. Cosmetics and 'good hair' will not enhance these qualities, nor will they mask the absence of them.

Note: the area under your bathroom sink is a magnet for clutter. Pull out all the superfluous cleaning products, rags, and sponges. Keep only what you use. Consolidate half-empty containers. Toss the empty ones.

The watchword for the bathroom is hygiene.

THE KITCHEN

As we all know, the kitchen functions as a place to store and prepare food. It is also a place where friends and family gather to cook, eat, and socialize. What we may sometimes forget is that the kitchen is the beating heart of the home, the place where our loved ones share food, dreams, heartbreak, and joy.

Its importance cannot be underestimated, so let's look at ways to create a Rich Minimalist kitchen.

Full disclosure: for me, the kitchen is a foreign land. I visit, but I am not a native. I am not fluent. I can function, but I am not qualified to comment at length and in detail. Luckily, I married a woman who is. As I contemplated 'the kitchen' as a section in this book, I called to my wife, who was in the real, actual kitchen.

The conversation between us went something like this . . .

"Honey?"

"Yes?"

"I'm writing a book on Minimalism."

"How lovely."

"If I was going to do something in the kitchen, what would you suggest I do?"

"I love you dearly, but I would suggest you not try to cook."

"I completely understand. But if someone needed to really revamp the kitchen, get rid of the excess, lean into a healthy diet with a productive routine, what should they do?"

"Well, first, you'd need to empty all the cabinets and drawers, see what you actually have, so you don't go out and buy things you don't need."

"Excellent idea."

"Then you group all of your items—utensils, mugs, pots, pans, containers. That helps you see where you've got duplicates and surplus."

"Of course."

"All of these suggestions are going to save people money and help the environment. You know that, right?"

"Absolutely."

"Purge the duplicates. Then limit the table settings. Nobody has place settings for twenty anymore."

"Gotcha."

"The single-use appliances are kind of out, too."

"What are those?"

"Hot dog cooker. Popcorn machine. Ice tea maker. Bread maker."

"Those are real things?"

"They are. Plastic containers are out, for the most part. For some reason, the lids always seem to get lost, and you've just got these plastic containers that don't really work for anything. Glass containers, however, are in."

"I've seen those in our kitchen. Glass containers with things in them."

"Yes. Beans, rice, oatmeal, sun dried tomatoes, herbs. We don't have a lot of pots and pans, either. You only need one or two of each to cook a meal."

"Are there things people need to do? Like on a regular basis?"

"Cleaning out the fridge every week is helpful. Less food is wasted. Methane from decomposing food is avoided."

"How does she know this stuff?"

"What?"

"Nothing!"

"And knowing what's in your pantry so you don't overbuy. Use up one container of food before opening another container of the same food."

"I do that with peanut butter."

"I love you anyway. People shouldn't use paper towels, paper napkins, paper plates, plastic utensils, plastic cups—"

"Barbarians!"

"Let's not be judgmental. Let's just say it's not the best use of money, and it's bad for the planet. We all should use cloth napkins and silverware. No plastic wrap. No plastic containers for leftovers. No teflon pots or pans."

"The coating is bad, right?"

"Yes, the coating is bad. Stainless steel is better. And you really only need one small appliance, not three or four."

"What's a small appliance?"

"A blender or a toaster."

"Got it. What about shopping?"

"I buy our rice and beans in bulk, which is more economical and saves on packaging, which is good for the environment. I also have an idea of what we're going to eat each week, and I only shop for those meals."

"We use a water filter pitcher!"

"We do! That saves on the expense of bottled water and the plastic bottles going in the trash, needing to be recycled."

"And I'm brewing my own tea at home, not paying retail at the cafe."

"Your sacrifice is an inspiration to us all."

"What else can people do?"

"Compost their food waste if they can. Avoid purchasing novelty gadgets that they see promoted on infomercials."

"I love the informercial guys. They have so much energy."

"Some appliances are more versatile, more multi-purpose than others. So checking that out can help."

"Like . . . ?"

"A dutch oven. An immersion blender."

"No idea what those are."

"Just write it down. Your readers will know."

"Any general menu advice?"

"Italian food, Indian food, and Chinese food are the best models to follow in the kitchen. It's easy to go vegetarian that way."

"Thank you, my love!"

"You're welcome, my darling."

Now that we've detailed the utensils and equipment you'll need in order to use this space efficiently, I should probably address a related issue.

Of course, Minimalism is the practice of reducing the number of possessions we own and reducing the amount of money we spend on unnecessary items. The Rich Minimalist philosophy expands upon this concept by introducing a financial component—becoming wealthier sooner by spending less. It also promotes the enjoyment of luxury in a responsible, refined manner.

Furthermore, this way of life also advocates minimizing our impact on the planet. Simply said, Rich Minimalists don't trash Mother Earth. Global warming is front and center in our daily lives. It impacts all of us and will impact future generations, especially if we don't change our current behaviors.

It's easy to point the finger at big-baller billionaires flying around the world in gas-guzzling private jets, or big-boned Bubba's driving around the country in gas-guzzling SUVs.

However, a serious contributor to global warming and a host of other environmental issues is far closer to home, and much easier to correct than we realize or want to admit. Adopting a plant-based diet, as opposed to a diet that includes animal products like cows, chickens, pigs, and fish, is an effective way to ease the strain on the planet . . . and live a healthier life.

If you're huffing, puffing or rolling your eyes at the previous statement, I'd encourage you to set aside what you're certain of and what you're familiar with. I'd encourage you to set aside what you think you're capable of. I'd encourage you to take a deep breath, keep an open mind, and do some quick, simple research.

Compare obesity rates, diabetes rates, cardiovascular disease rates, and cancer rates for the general population versus those who opt for a vegetarian or vegan diet. Visit the World Health Organization website. Review its list of carcinogens (cancer causing substances or agents). When you find 'processed meats' listed with 'cigarettes', think for a moment. Perhaps this information is new to you. Consider it.

Do a Google search for something like, 'how much water, feed, energy, and time does it take to produce the meat contained in one hamburger?' The answer? About 1500 gallons of water. For one hamburger. Then there's the 4.5 acres of land needed for each cow. The impact of deforestation to raise more cows and feed more cows. The energy costs of transportation—from farm to stockyard to grocery store to kitchen—it kind of adds up.

All of this environmental damage . . . so we can eat beef? The impact from the factory farming of chickens and fish is no less disturbing. So give it some thought. And consider eating fewer animal products.

The watchword for the kitchen is nourishment.

The Living Room

The living room may be the most open and public space in your residence. It functions as a place to relax, read, and socialize with family and friends. It may also be the space in which you work and exercise. Therefore, it is important to keep it lightly furnished, organized, and clean.

In order to enjoy your living room to the fullest, you should consider the following:

- a sofa or a loveseat—not both

- two armchairs

- a coffee table and/or a small end table

- a lamp or two

- a bookshelf or two for books, and

- a rug.

It is best if you acquire only the items listed above. A cluttered living room is an energy drain. Avoid overcrowding. The items listed above make it easier for you to assemble a living room conversation space. The sofa or loveseat face the two armchairs. The coffee table rests in between them. And they all sit on the rug.

Note: the living room is probably the first room you see as you enter your residence. It should 'rise up to greet you', as my wife says. The furnishings, decor, light, and colors should make you and your guests feel welcome, comfortable, and safe.

The Dining Room/Work Space

If you work at home (who doesn't?), you may need a dining table or kitchen table that doubles as a work station. This dining/work space may be in your kitchen or living room, depending upon the layout of your residence and your personal preference.

This space is populated by your desktop, laptop, tablet, and perhaps a printer, as well as any paperwork (documents and files) that tags along with your work product. Also in this space are your household documents (passports, birth and marriage certificates, tax records, bank statements, healthcare receipts, etc., ad infinitum.)

More and more of our personal documents can be stored in a digital format. Still, paper is a part of our lives. In order to be efficient and not make ourselves crazy, we must organize and retain these records.

The simplest way to do this is with boxes. Boxes with labels. Within each labeled box, place files. Each file has a label. Within each file are the relevant documents. Flash drives can be included as well. It really is that simple. It would be ideal if you assembled your boxes and files, labeled them, and kept them perfectly organized at all times.

A more likely scenario is that you will assemble your boxes and files and begin keeping everything in order. Then, life will intervene and you will end up simply dropping important documents into a handy tray. That tray will fill up. Each month you'll need to sort the papers in it and place them in their appropriate box and file. And you know what? That's just fine. Keep it generally organized until you have the time to get it specifically organized.

Make the time at least once a month to keep yourself organized.

If you do have your work station in your living room or what you designate as a dining room, it is important to do the following:

- use the 'box/file/label' system to keep things contained and organized,

- when you finish work each day, turn off your laptop or desktop,

- put all of your documents away—in a file or in a box,

- put the boxes or files away, on the floor, in a closet, out of sight,

- if you have a desktop computer, put a cover (plastic, fabric, or towel) over it to signal that 'work is over',

- if you have a desk lamp, turn it off, and

- leave work behind.

The watchword for this space is organization.

The Fitness Space

If you are living in a smaller space, it may be necessary for your daily physical exercise to take place in your living room. Again, this is fine. And again, it is critical to keep your exercise equipment—yoga mat, weights, etc.—in a closet or in a box while not in use.

An exception, of course, is the stationary bicycle or treadmill.

The watchword for this space is health.

No Television

As I may have mentioned before, television is not a part of The Rich Minimalist world. A television is an initial expense to acquire and an ongoing expense to receive (usually mediocre) programming. It also requires space, which is precious. Worse yet, it alters the focus of your living room in a negative way: toward it and away from your family, your guests, your books, and your quiet time.

Alternatives to watching broadcast television include watching entertainment programs and movies on your laptop or tablet. Paying a monthly subscription fee for Netflix or Apple TV is an expenditure, but it is less expensive than pay television. The trick is to limit your subscriptions (two are enough) and your screen time.

Furthermore, with most subscription services, you are exposed to little or no advertising. This makes living with less easier. You are also exposed to less sensationalism in the news. This reduces unnecessary worry and allows you to stay focused on your goals, not the media's headlines.

A Word About Cleanliness

It is critical to note that cleanliness is paramount in all your living spaces. Keeping your residence clean reduces the chances of infection and illness. It also creates a sensation of calm and order that contributes to the clarity, focus, and discipline that are necessary to create wealth.

This isn't just my opinion and experience; it is a fundamental teaching of Hinduism, the world's oldest religions, as well as the ancient Chinese practice of Feng Shui. So let's not ignore thousands of years of wisdom. Let's keep it minimal, and let's keep it clean.

Set aside Saturday mornings to clean house.

A Final Note on the Living Room

The living room is the most versatile and the perhaps the busiest room in the house. We tend to walk through the living room often. We may eat, work, exercise, and take the occasional nap (!) in the living room.

Therefore, again, it is essential to keep the living room minimally furnished. This will make it easier to clean and easier to transition from one function to the other if necessary.

The watchword for the living room is relaxation.

A Note Regarding the 'Go Bag'

Sadly, we live in uncertain times.

Natural disasters (the 2025 fires in Pacific Palisades, California) and political uncertainty (all over the world) require us to consider the 'once unthinkable' as the 'now possible.' While I am not paranoid, I am realistic.

Furthermore, I live in a global community. Several of my neighbors here in Paris have had to flee their native lands, often quickly and with very little money, to start their lives over.

We should let their experience be our lesson—not to live in fear—but to prepare with awareness. Unforeseen events are a part of life. To be prepared to leave your home quickly, with essential documents and enough money and clothing to survive for a few days or weeks, is not a crazy idea. With that unpleasant reality in mind, let's take one rational, easy-to-implement step.

Somewhere in your residence, you need to keep a small duffle bag, carry-on bag, or backpack, fully packed and ready to go, that contains the following:

- Your passport
- Your birth certificate
- Cash in small bills
- A change of clothing or two
- A water bottle.
- A phone charger
- A flashlight
- A small first aid kit
- A hygiene kit with toothbrush, toothpaste, etc.
- A stock of prescription medications (refresh these regularly)
- Easy to pack, non-perishable food items: energy bars, etc. (refresh these regularly)

An online search for 'go bag essentials' will offer you more information than you may ever need. Consider the list above as a solid, reliable start.

If you live in an urban or suburban area, think more about surviving for a period of time in another country and less about surviving outdoors in the wilderness.

If you have cash you'd like to protect, you may consider an offshore bank account. Again, there are infinite resources online about this. Know your country's laws and regulations regarding foreign bank accounts. Be thorough. Be smart.

While this is not technically a 'minimalist' issue, I would feel negligent if I didn't include it in this book, considering the current political climate.

SUMMARY

In this chapter we addressed the functions of the main rooms in your residence. We also detailed the essential furnishings that are commonly found in each room.

The bedroom is the place where you go to sleep, to dress, to be alone with your thoughts, and to be intimate.

The bathroom is the place you go in order to keep yourself clean.

The kitchen is the place you go in order to nourish yourself with healthy food, and to connect with friends and family.

The living room is the place you go in order to relax, and to spend time socializing with friends and family.

Your work space, your spiritual space, and your fitness space may be contained within any of these rooms. This depends upon your personal preference and the layout of your residence.

Cleanliness is essential to The Rich Minimalist philosophy. All of these areas must be kept clean.

Exercise: scan home decor magazines and online images to determine the furnishings, fabrics, colors, and styles that resonate with you. Find a theme or time period (traditional, modern, French Country, oriental, art deco, etc.) that you feel is 'you'.

Build a vision board of images. Slowly—over several years—acquire only the very best and most essential pieces in order to elegantly, richly, and minimally furnish your residence.

Think about a 'Go Bag' containing essential documents and travel items should you need to leave your residence quickly.

How to Assess the Value of Material Possessions

A silly man wanted a better life, so he bought new clothes, hopeful his world would be different.

A simple man wanted a better life, so he moved to another city, hopeful his world would be different.

A wise man wanted a better life, so he educated himself, certain he would be different.

Full disclosure: I am not a fan of the 'quick fix'. Personal tendencies are usually deeply engrained in us and take awareness, effort, and time to correct. Watching others try to change long-held habits (usually involving diet, exercise, work, beliefs, or attitudes), I have rarely seen grand proclamations, new year's resolutions, 'hacks', or shortcuts endure. They've rarely worked for other people, and, candidly, they've rarely worked for me.

We must accept the fact that drastic changes are seldom well-thought-out. They are often emotional and reactionary. At best, the change in behavior is temporary, leaving us feeling bad about ourselves for failing to permanently improve. At worst, the repercussions of such a sudden change can prove worse than the original problem we were trying to solve.

So let's be realistic. Let's be thoughtful. Let's be deliberate. Let's be thorough. Let's avoid dogma. Let's be flexible in pursuit of steadfast goals, but let's commit to achieving those goals.

With those thoughts in mind, let's consider something very important to you, as someone who has resolved to adopt and embrace The Rich Minimalist philosophy: the true value of the things you presently own. This assessment is important because you don't want to discard things that you actually need and use. You don't want to get rid of things that would be costly to replace. Conversely, you don't want to labor under any illusions: most of the stuff you own has very little real value, as you will soon see. So we must strike a balance here.

Second full disclosure: I abhor waste. If I own something, it is because I use it on a regular basis. Nothing just sits, collecting dust. With that in mind, I would encourage you to consider the true value of the things you own as you think about getting rid of them. This 'value' comes in several forms. We must examine and understand all of them as we reduce the quantity of our material possessions wisely.

EMOTIONAL VALUE

Emotional value is quite simply the sentimental value that something has. Common items that carry large emotional value include:

- photos
- keepsakes
- jewelry
- family heirlooms, and
- travel souvenirs.

These items often retain powerful emotional value long after any material value has disappeared. My advice: if you have small items with strong emotional value, keep them for now. Put them in a what we'll call a Chaos and Confusion Box, and stick the box in your closet. Circle back to the box later, after you've addressed the bigger issues and ideas in this book.

However, if you have an unused automobile that has large emotional value, well, you're going to have to think about that. Automobiles and other large personal items take up space, require money to maintain and operate, demand attention, and consume resources that could otherwise be put to better use.

Know this: emotional attachment to high-maintenance, non-incoming producing items can be costly, psychologically and financially. You must find a productive way to address the items and the emotions.

STREET VALUE

When you consider donating something or tossing it in the trash, you may realize that the item might have value to others. It's possible you can sell it and realize a profit, or you may sell it and get a fraction of the retail price.

The 'street value', or what you could realize from the sale of an item at a garage sale or online, is a sometimes real factor. This is most common with the following items:

- name brand handbags
- gold or diamond jewelry
- name brand wristwatches and
- garments made by established, high-end brands that are still in good condition.

Thankfully, you can now look online and in a matter of minutes calculate how much money you might be able to get for your items. Once you know the price, you can determine if it's worthwhile to list the item, spend time interacting with potential buyers, ship the item, and then get paid.

Unless you're trying to sell an authentic Louis Vuitton handbag for thousands of dollars, it's often better to just give the things away and move on. It's rarely worth your time to try to sell things.

Note: know the Street Value before you pay the Retail Price. This difference will give you an idea of an item's real worth. This comparison will give you a moment to consider. A moment to avoid a bad purchase. A moment to keep more of your money in your pocket.

Replacement Value

When you consider tossing unused or unwanted items, you may want to calculate what it will cost you to replace the item if you need it in the future. Some people hesitate to the extreme and never throw anything out. Don't be one of those people. But do consider the replacement cost of an item if you use it frequently or occasionally.

I do not have a list for Replacement Value, as the items that will appear on it will be highly individual. My only advice here is to consider wisely.

Convenience Value

Let's face it: some material things are very convenient to have and use. They make our daily tasks much easier and even enjoyable. Even as I promote The Rich Minimalist philosophy, I realize that having a mobile phone is a convenience that now borders on a necessity. Having a landline phone is a convenience that borders on a redundancy.

Here, we walk up to a line—the edge of 'convenience'—and look to the other side of that line—which is the beginning of 'consumerism.' Yes, things make life convenient. It is our challenge to differentiate between what makes life easier and what makes us lazier.

There are no simple answers or fast formulas for this issue. However, when in doubt, be inconvenienced a little and live with less. You'll become more resourceful and may discover that something you thought you 'needed' wasn't really essential at all.

PROFITABILITY OR PRODUCTIVITY VALUE

There is a value beyond convenience: an item's Profitability or Productivity Value. This is a critical value to understand. Thankfully, it is usually an easy value to quantify.

Simply stated, when an item helps us be more productive or more profitable, we must retain that item. For example:

- if you are the owner of an online business, obviously you need a computer and internet access.

- if you work as a diplomat, you need a serious— perhaps expensive—wardrobe.

- if you operate a delivery business, you need a reliable vehicle.

- if you work at a factory, you do not need a serious wardrobe, but you still need to look presentable.

- if you live within 5 miles of your workplace, you may not need a car, but you may still need to get around town quickly.

Be more than honest with yourself here: be hard on yourself. "Does this item make me money?" "Does this item contribute to my productivity?" Obviously, if you cut wood for a living, a chainsaw is an item that makes you money. Less obviously, a stationary bike may be an item that contributes to your productivity, keeping you healthy through exercise, refreshed during long hours of work.

Determine the Profitability and the Productivity Value of each item you own. If you keep it, make sure you are using it to create value, not just to waste time and take up space.

Value Lost Through Retention

As I've mentioned before, holding onto things we don't need or really even want can be costly. There's the emotional drag of clutter, of course. There can also be the monetary costs of storage fees for items we never use or even see. Money wasted on a fishing boat or motorcycle that is only used twice a year could be money used to save, invest, and secure your financial independence.

Any perceived value that you think something might have must be weighed against the value lost by holding onto it, what we call the holding costs or maintenance costs. The biggest cost is opportunity cost. What could I have done with my money, my personal space, and my time if I had just had the courage to let things go? This is a question you don't want to ask yourself ten years from now. This is motivation to take smart, deliberate action now.

Summary

Assess the true value of every item you own. Embrace the Essential. Prioritize Profitability and Productivity. Question Convenience. Consider Street Value. Know the Costs of Retention. Discard the Superfluous.

Exercise: Enter a room of your residence. Look at all of the flat surfaces, beginning with the floor. Consider every item on every flat surface. Label it with a post-it note that reads E for essential, P for profitable and/or productive, and C for convenient. In your bedroom, for example, look at your bed. Label that E for essential, of course. You need a place to sleep.

Next, look at the golf clubs in the corner. The ones you haven't used in a year. Essential? No. Profitable or productive? Hardly. Convenient? Not at all. Street value? Marginal. Cost of retention? Minimal, but still . . . Get rid of them.

If you can't bring yourself to give it away, at least put it away, out of sight. Come back to it later with more resolve.

Remember: in roughly 90% of your residence, you want your flat surfaces to be empty and clean.

How to Retreat from Material Possessions

Make yourself small and resist.

There are some battles in life which require you to attack and conquer the enemy. To be a Rich Minimalist, however, you must adopt a different strategy. To be victorious, you must retreat and resist. Let me explain.

The outside world is full of temptations that require your attention and money to sustain themselves and profit. Consumer products are marketed relentlessly via billboards, magazines, newspapers, television, and social media. Succumb to their constant entreaties and you risk wasting time, losing focus, and squandering resources.

Furnished properly and protected wisely, your living space—whether it's a single room or a luxury residence—can act as your sanctuary from this chaotic outside world. It is your place to relax, study, contemplate, meditate, exercise, sleep, and be intimate.

Think of your residence as a palace, a temple, or a monastery. These can be helpful images, as they allow you to look around at your place and determine how much it resembles a palace, a temple, or a monastery. If you have clutter—which comes from the outside world—you have allowed the outside world into your sacred space.

You must establish boundaries. You must reclaim your territory. You must retreat from the distractions of the outside world. Because you are the target market for companies trying to sell you things, you must make yourself small by limiting your exposure to their efforts and resist their constant efforts to invade your mental and physical space. Only then can you obtain—and maintain—the clarity to make good decisions, decisions that benefit you.

Consider this scenario: someone is in distress. They are trying to get your attention. They need your help. Would you be likely to see them and come to their rescue quickly in a carnival with flashing lights, loud music, rides, and games? Or would you be more likely to see them and come to their rescue in, let's say, a church, where silence, sunlight, and serenity filled the space?

Of course, it would be easier to hear their pleas for help in the church. It's quiet. It's calm. It's serene. Now ask yourself this: what if you were the one crying for help? What if you were also the one who could help? Obviously, you'd want to be in the church and not at the carnival.

Being The Rich Minimalist helps you retreat from clutter and exterior distractions so you can, yes, hear your own cries for help, and help yourself. Only then will you be able to help others.

The ABC's of Retreat

There are a few things you can do to retreat from the bad carnival that is the Consumer World. These are obvious, simple steps that can have a profound impact on your living space and your mental space.

A is for Attrition: when something wears out or breaks, consider not replacing it. Ask yourself, Can I live without this? If you wait a week or two to decide, you'll have time to determine if you really need it, or if it was just something you thought would be nice to have.

B is for Box Up: place items that you're not using regularly in a box and store them out of sight for awhile. If you don't use them in 3 months or 6 months, it's time to donate them.

C is for Clean Out: empty your closets, drawers, cupboards, attic, and garage of obvious unused and unwanted items. Donate them or throw them in the trash. Go slowly, but make steady progress.

How To Resist

We live in a capitalist society. Most of the time, that's great. Entrepreneurs create products and services, inventions and innovations, filling needs and satisfying desires. Their businesses provide jobs, offer opportunities, and generate profits. These in turn contribute to tax revenues which provide social services. Our government can keep us safe, educate citizens, and help those in need.

You are a participant in this system. You earn an income, buy things, and pay taxes. If you spend as much as you earn—or more—you can become a victim of this system. You will have lots of stuff, but no savings, no investments, fewer options, and no independence. If you resist—that is, resist the temptation to purchase things you don't need—you can benefit from this system. You can generate an income, limit your expenditures, pay your taxes, then save and invest for the future, using the capitalist system to your advantage.

If we are to resist effectively, we must do so on several fronts.

Consumerism. We must resist consumerism. Buying things we don't need or too much of what we do need will only cost us money, robbing us of financial independence, opportunities, and options. Consumerism may also leave us emotionally unfulfilled, frustrated, and angry.

Display. We must resist display. Showing others how much wealth we have—or how much wealth we want others to think we have—only invites trouble, making us targets of criminals and fake friends. It also reveals our insecurities, which our adversaries can take advantage of.

Distraction. We must resist distraction. Television, social media, and gossip are the deserts of small minds. Education, books, and travel are the kingdoms of the truly wise. We must focus and minimize distraction.

Waste. We must eliminate waste in our daily lives. We must endeavor to be efficient and economical in the items we buy and the way we use them. We must also be aware of how we spend our time. We should not waste it.

Food for thought: we should go through life like a fish through water, being very selective about when and where we make a splash, if at all.

Summary

To make Minimalism effective and easy, it is best to gradually retreat from consumer culture, distraction, and waste.

We should make the most of the capitalist system we live in by working in it and earning an income. We should distance ourselves from it by limiting our exposure to advertising and propaganda. This will make it easier to limit our expenses. We can then leverage our savings, making the most of investment opportunities available to us.

Exercise: When you have a free moment and are tempted to open your phone and start scrolling, pause. Put your phone away. Sit for a moment. Think. Let your mind rest. What were you looking for on your phone? What is 'out there' that is more important than what's 'in here'? 'In here' being your heart and your mind.

Instead of scrolling, think about your plans for the future. How are they progressing? Think about your physical condition? Are you happy with it? Think about your emotional state. Are you feeling fulfilled?

None of these answers will be found on your phone. Only in frequent, quiet contemplation.

How to Prioritize Acquisitions

It is important that we do the right thing. It is important that we do the right thing well. It is most important that we do the right thing at the right time.

To be a Rich Minimalist is to reinvent your living space, refine your wardrobe, and improve your life. This chapter will help you prioritize acquisitions for your living space. This will help you avoid overbuying, overspending, and clutter. It will also, again, make it easier to get rid of unwanted, unhelpful, or obsolete items in your living space. So let's start with the most important considerations first, then we'll address the acquisition of material things.

First, if you are just starting out, you need to locate a safe, clean, and hopefully quiet place to live. I mention this because people sometimes start their search for a residence looking at the apartment complex's amenities, like the pool and health club, its proximity to 'nightlife', or the perceived status of a certain neighborhood.

None of these matter. What matters is finding a safe, clean residence, close to public transportation, close to your work, close to good schools, close to a farmers market. These are the things to prioritize.

Another factor to consider is the size (square footage or square meters) of your residence. While it's nice to have space, you will be paying for every square foot or square meter, as the size of a residence is a contributing factor to rental rates and home prices. So we'll be doing more with less for a very good reason. Money.

A key element of this Minimalism philosophy is, not surprisingly, maximizing your opportunities for financial independence. Therefore, the smaller the space you live in, the less you pay in rent, the more you save, the more you invest, the sooner you have options.

Obvious but important fact: it is easier to live in a smaller space when you live with less stuff.

Furnishing Your Place

Now that you've prioritized a clean, safe place to live that is smaller in size and less expensive, let's again review a list of the essential furnishings, presented in order of their importance.

For the bedroom:

- 1 bed

- 2 sets of bed linens (sheets and pillow cases)

- 1 blanket or comforter

- 2 nightstands

- 2 lamps

- 1 chest of drawers, if closet space is limited

- 1 rug, if needed.

My advice is to purchase the highest quality bed and bed linens that you can afford, even if you delay other acquisitions for a period of time. You're going to spend about 8 hours a day in bed. You need to wake up refreshed and ready to rock and roll, not exhausted or stiff from a poor night's sleep.

When shopping for sheets and pillow cases, look for high thread count, Egyptian cotton linens. Familiarize yourself with brands such as Quince, Ferette, and Matouk. Watch for sales.

For the bathroom:

- 1 set of bath towels

- 1 set of hand towels

- 1 set of wash cloths.

Again, opt for quality here. Watch for sales. This is an opportunity to enjoy a real luxury on a daily basis with huge, thick, and utterly divine bath sheets. And look for a luxurious bathrobe, as well.

For the dining area and kitchen:

- 1 dining table with 2 or 4 chairs
- 4 cloth napkins
- 4 plates
- 4 glasses
- 4 bowls
- 4 forks
- 4 knives
- 4 spoons
- Cooking utensils, such as spoon, spatulas, and cutting knife
- 3 pots
- 2 skillets

As I've mentioned, you'll want to avoid teflon coated pots and pans. Opt for stainless steel or iron. Again, take this opportunity to curate high-quality cookware and luxurious tableware for yourself. Go slowly. Opt for elegance.

For the living area:

- 1 sofa
- 2 armchairs
- 1 coffee table
- 2 floor lamps
- 1 rug

For furnishings in the living room (and other rooms), consider thrift shops and auction houses. They offer quality, pre-owned items at a fraction of the retail price you'd pay for new items. Also check online for individuals selling their furniture.

Remember: if you don't like the fabric color of an old sofa, you can always buy it inexpensively and then have it recovered. Avoid buying furniture off a showroom floor if at all possible.

Again, there is no television on The Rich Minimalist home furnishings list. There is no video game console on the list. Avoid these in order to live a richer life. Listen to music instead.

Pleasant surprise: being a Rich Minimalist, you are allowed to have as many books in your living space as you wish! Books and bookshelves take up a minimal amount of space while offering an infinite amount of wisdom, information, entertainment, and personal development opportunities.

SPECIAL SPACES

Remember, there are three small, special spaces within your overall living area that will be important for you to identify and maintain. These three spaces are your Work Space, your Fitness Space, and your Spiritual Space.

Your Work Space is the area that you use to work. This is the desk or table where you sit, open your laptop, and do your work. It may or may not include a printer. It may or may not include office supplies, paper files, or documents. The Work Space may or may not be always visible, with everything on the table. You can pull things out of a cabinet or drawer and do your work. When you're finished, you can put things away and use the same table and chair for dining.

The Fitness Space functions along the same lines. You can pull out a yoga mat and a pair of light weights, push your armchairs out of the way, do your workout, then put your equipment back in a closet or under the bed. Your living room quickly returns to being a living room after your workout.

Exception: the stationary bike may always be visible in your living room or in your bedroom. Be content with this. Be unapologetic about this. 30 minutes a day on a stationary bike can change your life. It is worth the space it takes in your residence. It is worth the daily effort.

The Spiritual Space, however, is different. As we discussed, it is a small altar, picture, table, or nightstand that holds your own personal spiritual statue, image, symbol, or meaningful items that remind you of your faith. Like your faith and your god(s), your Spiritual Space remains unchanging, steadfast, and constant.

Hindus have Ganesha and Lakshmi. Christians have Jesus and Mary. Buddhists have the Buddha. If you don't have an image or statue, simply set a candle on a small table and surround it with fresh fruit and flowers.

The purpose of the Spiritual Space is to provide a daily visual reminder of a Higher Power, whatever or whoever you believe that to be. This space will encourage you to be calm during hard times, grateful during good times, and stay on an even keel at all times.

Sure, everybody is busy. However, it is a good idea to start your day with a few minutes of prayer, mediation, or quiet contemplation in front of your altar, in your Spiritual Space, every morning.

It is also important to identify and separate the Work Space, the Fitness Space, and the Spiritual Space, even as you live in a smaller, cleaner, less-cluttered space. Work in one space. Exercise in one space. Pray or meditate in one place, even if these three spaces are in the same room.

A Quick Word

Even as you allow for roommates, spouses, partners, siblings, children, or parents, you can be the master of your living space. You can create your own personal sanctuary for sanity, your own joyful, welcoming space for entertaining, your own elegant atelier for creativity. You accomplish this through the mindful selection of material possessions, cleanliness, and organization.

Adding material possessions to your living space or wardrobe will not improve the quality of your life, make you more intelligent, or make you more attractive. Prioritizing productive activities in your living space can add to the quality of your life and may make you more intelligent and more attractive. It can also make you richer.

Prioritize work, reading, exercise, meditation, and joyful moments with friends and family. With fewer material possessions to clutter your place, it will be easier to keep your residence clean. It will also be easier to think about what you want and need to do. It will be easier to then do it. Note: as you reduce the amount of 'stuff', the energy in your living space will elevate and expand.

You now have a list of the furnishings you need in order to live The Rich Minimalist life. If you already have your residence furnished, you can use the list above to reduce the number of material possessions in your living space.

Remember: clean, flat surfaces. Comfortable, functional furnishings. Room to think. Room to breathe. Room to be.

Summary

Your living space is your personal space. It simultaneously reflects your inner world and supports it. You must prioritize the acquisition of material possessions on a 'needs first' basis, then carefully consider what items to add from there.

When you consider your bed, bed linens, and tableware, opt for quality and even luxury.

Chinese proverb: buy the best and you only cry once.

Your Special Spaces are your Work Space, your Fitness Space, and your Spiritual Space. Designate these spaces. Keep them organized and clean.

Exercise: Determine which room or area is going to contain your Work Space, Fitness Space, and Spiritual Space. Practice only the dedicated activity in that space every day for one week.

How does it feel? Is your altar in the right place? Is your 'office' in the right place? Are you exercising in the right place?

Adjust as needed.

How to Curate Your Signature Look

At the Cafe of Style, Elegance can often be found in a corner, whispering with Simplicity.

Previously, I offered advice about how to reduce the number of garments in your wardrobe. Streamlining your wardrobe helps you in a number of ways:

- It eliminates decision fatigue, making it easier to pull together a great look effortlessly every day, selecting from a limited number of quality pieces that are both classic in style and versatile in function.

- It reduces the number of clothes in your closet, creating more storage and living space, and freeing up the energy in your residence.

- It offers you the space to acquire books, exercise equipment, or other tools that will enhance your quality of life and help you make more money.

- It creates opportunities for others who shop at charity or thrift stores to buy your good used clothing at affordable prices.

First, it is important to discard unwanted or obsolete garments and live for awhile with your reduced and somewhat refined wardrobe. Only after a period of time do you begin curating your Signature Look based upon Rich Minimalist fundamentals.

Note: this is not an excuse to go shopping. This is a slow process which will help you refine your image and curate a wardrobe that reflects a new, more sophisticated You. Before we discuss garments or style, we must address The Rich Minimalist criteria for your garment purchases.

They are as follows:

- Your clothes should be easy on the wallet. This does not mean cheap. This means that you can afford them. You can pay cash for them. It also means that you prioritize quality. This ensures that you invest in clothes. When you do, they last longer, saving you money.

- Your clothes should be easy on the eye. This does not mean plain. This means each item should easily mix and match with most of the other items in your wardrobe, and they should be classic—not trendy—in style.

- Your clothes should be easy on the maintenance. This means you're able to wash and dry most of your clothes yourself, without the expense of dry cleaning. Consider a handheld steamer instead, and learn to iron your own garments.

- Your clothes should be easy on the planet. Buying a ten dollar t-shirt that falls apart in six months is disastrous on a couple of fronts: first, it was most likely made in a sweatshop, where vulnerable people work in horrid conditions for unfair wages. Second, the cheap garment will probably end up in a landfill, choking our already over-taxed planet.

Note: I first addressed getting rid of your old clothes in Chapter 4. I did not return to the subject of curating a new style for yourself until this chapter, much later in the book. I did this for two reasons.

First, you need time to let information sink in. Only after contemplation can you take deliberate, effective action. Advising you to discard clothing in one chapter, then go out and buy clothing in the next chapter doesn't make much sense. You need time to think in between.

Second, too many people think that Minimalism is just about the clothes, specifically wearing black t-shirts and black jeans seven days a week. It's not. So let's maintain a 360-degree perspective, even as we address clothing again. Let's take a look at two different groups who have already mastered The Rich Minimalist wardrobe.

THE PARISIANS

Our French friends have been minimalists for decades.

They have mastered the fundamentals of living well with fewer items (and in smaller spaces), more often out of necessity than anything else.

If you paid attention during history class, you'll remember that post World War II France was not an affluent place overall. Paris, in particular, was just finding its feet economically. People lived in small apartments (and still do), and many had little in the way of disposable income.

Parisians, however, are a breed apart, and nothing if not resourceful and stylish. Rising from the ashes, as it were, they quickly embraced an economical, functional, and elegant wardrobe philosophy that has been imitated the world over by rich and poor alike.

That philosophy is, quite simply, Black. Coco Chanel made a fortune with The Little Black Dress. French writers made a statement with the black turtleneck sweater. Today, the tailored black suit with a fitted white shirt or blouse is The Uniform for Parisians. Egalitarian, anonymous, timeless, and versatile.

The navy blue suit with a white shirt or blouse is a second popular option, but it doesn't have the gravitas of *le costume noir*. The only variables in this option are the quality of the suit, the quality of the shirt or blouse, and the quality of the shoes.

While many people are desperate to communicate their ambitions, background, and tribe with their choice of clothing, this ensemble gives away nothing. There is no message, only mystery. It's not preppy. It's not goth. It's not hip-hop. It's not anything. It's just a black suit, or a black sweater over a white shirt with a black pair of jeans and white sneakers. Worn well, this Black is anything but basic.

I know Parisian men who wear nothing but black suits, black jackets, black sweaters, and black jeans . . . all with white dress shirts. And they look great. All the time. I kind of resent them. I kind of admire them. But, you know, that's very Parisian. So I'm okay with these feelings.

The Parisian women follow suit, so to speak, opting occasionally for the colorful scarf to add a little flair.

As a Rich Minimalist, Black is your first option. There are, however, a few things to keep in mind:

- Wearing all black all the time may make you depressed. If it does, opt for another style or include the white shirt or blouse.

- Black jeans fade if you wash and dry them too harshly or too often. It's not a great look.

- Lint and the fur of white animals will become your mortal enemies.

- Summer months with hot temperatures can be challenging.

- Be careful not to take yourself too seriously. It's just Black.

Know this: if you decide to dress Parisian Black, the quality and fit of the garments you choose will be telling. You will own fewer garments. Therefore, they will need to be very well made. You will most likely spend more, less often. In doing so, however, you will come out ahead financially and impress all the right people with your style.

THE OLD MONEY CROWD

The second group who have consciously or unconsciously embraced Minimalism with their wardrobe choices are the Old Money folks.

These people have grown up with serious privilege. Their world is one of trust funds, boarding schools, summer cottages, and private clubs. Always discreet and often unassuming, they are the walking, talking embodiment of generational wealth. They don't need to impress anyone, especially with the way they dress, but they still *communicate* with the way they dress.

The Old Money Guys (and some Gals) are often seen wearing an oxford cloth button down dress shirt with chinos and penny loafers. If it's a more formal occasion, the Guys will wear a blue blazer, tweed jacket, grey wool slacks, and perhaps a rep tie. These garments, coupled with a wool sweater, corduroys, or LL Bean ankle boots for cooler, wetter weather, comprise the fundamental uniform of an Old Money Guy.

For the Old Money Gals, think pastel blouses, wool or cotton sweaters, khakis, wool pants, and wool skirts. Deck shoes, penny loafers, and practical chunk heels are the Gals' footwear of choice.

The Old Money look is not really 'preppy' in the 21st century sense of the word. It's now known as Ivy Style on the internet, if you seek a visual frame of reference. The origins of this ensemble can traced from British boarding schools, then to the New England prep schools and Ivy League universities in 1950s America.

Like Parisian Black, this look is functional, egalitarian, anonymous, timeless, and versatile. In this uniform, you're appropriately dressed for a sales call or a pub crawl. It matters not. This option is not 'big logos and pretense'. This option is 'tradition and discretion'. The Old Money wardrobe might have a more relaxed fit than Parisian Black, but the timelessness and practicality of this option are undeniable.

A Few Thoughts

With either of these choices—Parisian Black or Old Money Style—you can curate a great looking wardrobe that fulfills your professional obligations and meshes with your personality . . . for not a lot of money. You'll acquire a limited number of quality garments. You'll spend less overall. Your biggest challenge? Curating this new wardrobe slowly and patiently, paying cash, and knowing when to stop.

Rich Minimalist Rule: once you've acquired the perfect number of garments to get you through a week or two, you need to stop shopping for clothes. After that, whenever you buy a new article of clothing, you need to get rid of an existing garment of clothing. One in, one out. This discipline will help you limit the number of garments you acquire, even if they match your Parisian Black or Old Money aesthetic.

Rich Minimalist Timeframe: allow yourself 12 months to transition fully from your existing wardrobe into a new minimalist style. Discard deliberately, purchase wisely.

Rich Minimalist Strategy: adopting Minimalism as a way of life is something you might want to do on the down-low, as they say. I wouldn't tell anyone what you're doing. Just let the change appear gradually—in your wardrobe, your personal space, and your life. If someone asks, just shrug off the new look or new choices as an offhand, minor thing you decided to do. No big deal.

Rich Minimalist Secret: rarely let others know what you're thinking. It will make your plans easier to consider, implement, refine, complete, and enjoy.

Rich Minimalist Reality: Minimalism requires maintenance. You'll probably have to go into your closet and drawers once or twice a year and discard unwanted or unused items.

The price of liberty is eternal vigilance. (Not my quote, sadly.)

Summary

As you curate your Signature Look, consider Parisian Black or Old Money Style. Both are timeless. Both can be assembled with very few garments. Both are easy to mix and match. Both are easy to maintain.

At its best, Parisian Black includes the white dress shirt or white blouse and black jacket, black pants, with black dress shoes (or white sneakers). This is a versatile, economical, and elegant choice. The black t-shirt and black jeans combo is a classic, but too often the garments are not of good quality, and the look suffers as a result.

Old Money Style is timeless. An oxford cloth button down long sleeve dress shirt, a pair of chinos, and penny loafers or deck shoes has been a go-to ensemble for almost a century. Don't expect that to change any time soon. This choice is easy to mix, match, and upgrade with the blue blazer, tweed jacket, wool sweater, and wool pants. When in doubt about colors, default to blue, grey, tan, and brown.

Exercise: Click on Google Images and search for '20th century style icons'. Among the results you may find Jackie Kennedy, Coco Chanel, Katherine Hepburn, Cary Grant, Princess Diana, and others. Look at their simple, comfortable, and elegant ensembles. If it's helpful, follow the example of a style icon as you curate your Signature Look.

Note: if you work from home (telecommute), you still need to get dressed each day, as if you were going into the office. Studies have shown that people are more alert and productive after they take a shower, shave and/or put on some makeup, and get dressed for the day.

How to Redefine Luxury

Some people think luxury is the opposite of poverty. It is not. It is the opposite of vulgarity. - Coco Chanel

Make no mistake: being a Rich Minimalist means enjoying Luxury. Not a typo, my friend. Luxury with a capital 'L'. This may seem illogical or contradictory . . . until we begin to look at Luxury differently. It is important to see Luxury as an experience, not a product or service. Yes, it is often a product or service, but these are only the tangible representations or expressions of the concept.

We are all familiar with a Luxury that we purchase and enjoy only once—usually the moment we pay for it. However, the best Luxury is the one that we enjoy over and over again, even if we've only paid for it once. What's more, as we shall soon learn, we enjoy quite a few things that we may not consider Luxuries.

So let's expand and refine our definition of Luxury. As we do, we'll be able to live a more luxurious life on a daily basis.

A Little Lesson in Luxury

At its best, Luxury is an experience which gives us an immersive emotional response—a sense of pleasure, satisfaction, fulfillment, joy. It can come in the form of a foot massage. It can be the moment we slip into a cashmere sweater. It can be the aroma of a fine perfume. Because it is emotional, true Luxury therefore originates in our mind.

First, there is the state of awareness, to understand that what we are experiencing is wonderful and extraordinary. This is not routine. This is not commonplace. This is not mediocre. This is not an afterthought. This is the very best.

Second, there is an informed understanding of the experience—we comprehend the unique nature of the craftsmanship, the expertise, the materials, the presentation, the tradition.

Third, there is appreciation, the feeling of gratitude that someone conceived and created this Luxury, and that we are alive and able to enjoy it.

Fourth, there is freedom from worry, the confidence that we can enjoy the Luxury without being concerned about its price. This final freedom is only present when we have prioritized correctly, when we have placed working, saving, and investing before shopping, buying, and owning.

Remember: true Luxury is personal. A Luxury for one person may not mean a thing to another person.

For example, I have no idea why anyone would pay $5000.00 for a bicycle. The design, engineering, construction, and performance of a high-end bicycle are not things I appreciate or understand. Therefore, an expensive bicycle is not a Luxury for me, but it is for many other people.

If you are to enjoy Luxury fully, you need to be honest with yourself about which products, services, or experiences resonate with you. You can't be influenced by what advertisers have told you is a Luxury. Only you can determine individually and independently which product, service, or experience is a Luxury for you.

THE TEN RICH MINIMALIST LUXURIES

Now that you understand these concepts, let's take a look at a few things you may not have considered to be Luxuries.

Health. It's difficult to be productive and enjoy anything if you don't feel well. Ask someone with a chronic illness if they'd like to be healthy or if they'd like a new wristwatch. The answer won't surprise you.

Likewise, someone who is emotionally unhealthy will want to be happy before anything else. They just may seek happiness in shopping, sex, alcohol, or drugs, or pursue those as a way to compensate for the lack of it. If we are healthy, we're experiencing a daily Luxury for which we should be grateful. We should also prioritize our diet and exercise routines in order to preserve our health, to consistently enjoy this most important Luxury.

Peace. Waking up each day in a place without bombs dropping or armies invading is a Luxury that millions of people don't enjoy. If we are lucky enough to live in a relatively peaceful environment, we should consider that a real Luxury.

Peace is also peace of mind. This Luxury is often the result of our thoughts, words, and actions being in complete alignment with each other. We are not troubled by conflicting agendas, mixed emotions, or divided loyalties. We are not plagued by contradictions. We are comfortable with our choices, which are based on principles, not circumstances.

Freedom. Coming and going as we please, speaking our minds, and doing pretty much what we want to do in the pursuit of happiness . . . this kind of freedom is a Luxury, and one we should not take for granted or abuse.

Freedom is also freedom from worry, to not be concerned about what other people think or what might happen tomorrow, next week, or next year. Yes, we plan ahead and do our best to prepare, but we allow our minds to be free in the moment and enjoy this freedom as a Luxury.

Safety. Being able to walk the street and sleep at night in relative safety and security is a Luxury, especially to those who don't have it.

There is also a certain safety in being financially independent. If we have enough money, we can feel safe in the midst of turbulent economic conditions. However, if we are not financially secure, we must work to create a mental and emotional state of faith, of knowing that we are safe, no matter what happens.

Family and Friends. Having someone we can confide in when times are tough—or howl with when things are ridiculous—is more than a Luxury. It's a priceless treasure. Yes, our family and friends get on our nerves, but if we recognize and appreciate those magic moments of laughter, joy, and celebration, we realize how often the good outweighs the bad.

Loving Our Work. Enjoying what we do for a living is a Luxury that 95% of the people in this world don't experience, regardless of how much money they make. Some are 'okay' with their jobs. Others barely tolerate their workplace and try to shove all of their 'living' into weekends. As a result, they tend to be less happy, spending more money to compensate.

If we can do what we love for work, money is a by-product. Satisfaction is our reward. We work as an act of service, ,and we live Luxuriously, regardless of our income.

Financial Independence. Not being obligated to go to work is a huge Luxury. Of course, work—in whatever form it takes—is essential to happiness. It is having the freedom to select the terms of the endeavor that matter. No material possession feels as good as financial independence. Embracing The Rich Minimalist philosophy will accelerate our progress toward financial independence and minimize the discomfort of any sacrifices we need to make in order to achieve it.

Charity. Being able to give to others is a fundamental part of being human and a great feeling, too. The true Luxury is to be able to give often, spontaneously, and generously, expecting nothing in return.

Our giving is not only financial. We can be kind, patient, and generous of spirit, especially to those who can do nothing to us or for us.

Public Service. To be in a position to serve our fellow citizens is an important Luxury. If we have the capacity, inclination, and opportunity, we must serve our fellow man in public office.

This is often a thankless endeavor, with few definitive victories and seemingly constant setbacks. Still, making the world a better place, even in a small way, is a vital contribution to society.

Legacy. To leave a legacy, whether it be an inheritance of cash or a forest of newly planted trees, is a tremendous Luxury for us . . . and a tremendous blessing for generations to come. It is a powerful and wonderful feeling to say, 'I have plenty. So, here, take this and enjoy it with my best wishes.'

THE ONE WELL-CHOSEN LUXURY

Years ago, when I lived in Los Angeles, I would frequent a Westwood cigar store on Saturday mornings. The usual gang of regulars would amble in, styrofoam cups of coffee in hand. A dozen bagels from the shop next door always seemed to magically appear. Cigars would be purchased, cut, and lit.

For the next hour or two, we'd loiter with intent—talking, laughing, complaining, and pontificating. The Lakers, the kids, the in-laws, the job. The usual.

Some of the guys were multimillionaire Hollywood writers. Some were selling office supplies. More relevant to our discussion was this fact: some of the guys I hung out with would never pay more than thirty bucks for a shirt or pay more than ten bucks for a haircut. They watched every dime in their daily lives. Still, they had no problem paying fifty bucks for a contraband Cuban cigar once or twice a month. They were perfectly happy to watch money, literally, go up in smoke. Why? Because it was the cigar—and the socializing that went along with it—that was really enjoyable and meaningful to them.

It was their One Well-Chosen Luxury.

Like many truly luxurious moments, it contained more than one component: it was the cigar, but it was also the camaraderie. I encourage you to take this same approach to Luxury.

Consider the following best practices as you do:

- Your Luxury should have a deep, immersive, emotional resonance for you. It may mean nothing to others, but for you it's the cat's meow.

- Your Luxury shouldn't require a lot of maintenance or overhead. Think of what's involved in taking care of a cashmere scarf (dry cleaning) as opposed to what's involved in taking care of a vintage Ferrari (storage, insurance, repairs . . .).

- You should be able to pack your Luxury in a suitcase and walk with it (product), or enjoy it anywhere in the world (service).

- You should be able to enjoy your Luxury over and over again, if possible, after a single initial financial outlay.

- If your Luxury isn't a one-time purchase that results in repeated enjoyment, it's best if it is only a nominal expense at varying intervals, like a manicure, a massage, or, yes, a Cuban cigar.

Very Important Note: if you're in a romantic relationship, you should know your partner's One Well-Chosen Luxury. Give it as a birthday or anniversary gift. Make sure they have the opportunity to fully enjoy it.

A Little Luxury Safari

If you haven't found your One Well-Chosen Luxury just yet, or if that particular Luxury is out of reach financially for you right now, consider going on a Little Luxury Safari for some smaller, daily pleasures.

Here are a few Luxuries to explore, curate, and enjoy:

Fragrance. If you've found the fragrance or cologne that really resonates with you, then you know what a Luxury the right scent can be. Enjoy it. If you haven't found that particular fragrance, it's time to go on Little Luxury Safari.

Visit a cosmetics boutique near you to try a few scents, or check online for sample kits from established vendors. Both approaches offer free or inexpensive ways to discover the fragrance that's right for you.

Remember: fragrance is not limited to your body. A pleasant aroma in your home is also key. Explore top quality room diffusers and incense to give a calm, prosperous feel to your living room, bedroom, and bathroom.

Once you've found the fragrance that really speaks to you, save up and invest in it.

Bath Soap. Bath soap is one of those under-appreciated Luxuries. An entire universe of scents and ingredients awaits you. Consider the centuries-old Savon de Marseille, a traditional soap handmade in France. Originally made from olive oil (now vegetable oil formulas are available), it may be better for your skin than mass-produced soaps. It certainly is more Luxurious.

Plants. Fresh flowers and lush houseplants inject life into minimally furnished rooms. You don't have to pay super-retail prices at your local florist. Investigate your local wholesale flower market. Find out if you can access their facilities and buy from their vendors.

Learn how much light and water certain plants need, and select according to your home's design . . . and according to your commitment to take care of them. Only buy plants that you're going to take care of. Dead or dying plants are not part of The Rich Minimalist home.

Candles. Nothing sets a mood like candles. If you want to sit in solitude and meditate, nothing provides tranquility and focus like a single flame, flickering in the dark. If you want to connect with your partner, nothing promotes intimacy like a bedroom bathed in the glow of candlelight.

Explore scented and unscented candles. You don't have to spend a lot. Check online and in discount stores. Consider supporting artisan candlemakers in your area.

Coffee and Tea. One of life's simple pleasures that is perhaps much more appreciated here in Europe than in the United States is the enjoyment of quality coffee and tea. Mega-brands like Starbucks and Lipton dominate street corners and grocery store shelves. Exposed to little else, many people think they're drinking 'great' coffee and 'refreshing' tea. They most likely are not.

Explore coffee from Tazza d'Oro. Taste the smoothness of Marco Polo tea from Mariage Freres, or the Weekend in Paris blend from Damann Freres. Learn how to properly prepare a quality hot beverage. Brew a cup at home. Sit back, sip, and savor. Like fragrance, flowers, houseplants, and candles, think of your search for great coffee and tea as another Little Luxury Safari.

So, with friends or alone, embark on an adventure. Set a budget for yourself. See how much Luxury you can get for your money.

Luxury as a Tool

Please know that I am very careful to avoid dogma. While I think it is important to live a life based on integrity and honesty, I am keenly aware that we live in the real world. Shades of grey abound.

That said, let me articulate this reality: some material possessions communicate success, sophistication, influence, and expertise to other people. In certain circumstances, owning certain material possessions can communicate these abilities and attributes, even if one does not possess them entirely. Owning these things and using them to communicate in order to gain the confidence of colleagues and clients can be effective. It can help in the accomplishment of your goals.

In this context, a material possession can be what we'll call a 'communications tool' or a 'social tool'. These tools can be effective because, in short, people judge. They draw conclusions based on appearances. Being aware of this reality can be useful, if you are wise.

An example: a young investment advisor I know had achieved a certain level of success. Still, she wanted to attract more clients, and she wanted clients who had more money to invest. She contacted me and asked for my advice. (I am the author of *The Old Money Book*).

She wondered how she might communicate the success she'd achieved so far without falling into the trap of conspicuous consumption. She wanted to communicate her confidence and expertise to potential clients, nonverbally and discreetly. She also admitted that she wanted to reward herself (a little) for the professional stature that she'd achieved so far.

Her candor and awareness were impressive. She 'knew her audience', and she was smart to be cautious. I suggested that she purchase a small, classic, stainless steel Cartier tank wristwatch. With its black leather band and plain white face, it is the least expensive watch the company makes.

Nevertheless, it whispers sophistication, elegance, and a certain level of success. In this context, an item typically considered a Luxury is now a business tool. This material possession is useful, but only if accompanied by skill, professionalism, and performance.

The investment advisor now wears her Cartier watch. She continues to serve her clients well. She attracts new, more affluent clients who note her abilities and track record . . . and maybe the wristwatch.

Remember these criteria for an effective 'communications tool' or 'social tool':

- You can easily afford it, meaning you can pay cash and not sweat it.
- It is economical to own (low or no maintenance).
- It is discreet and appropriate for the work culture.
- It is effective with the intended audience.

Furthermore, this 'communications tool' is never referred to or bragged about by the owner. It is allowed to communicate on its own, nonverbally, and it is always accompanied by world class effort and stellar results. When a luxury item outshines its owner or overpromises in its implications, it is a distraction and a liability.

Remember: wearing a gold Rolex will not make you a famous rapper. Driving a Mercedes Benz will not make you a successful real estate agent. However, at a certain point, some material possessions can be useful tools in your professional life.

As with all 'things', their acquisition requires us to be honest with ourselves about our motivation. As with all 'things', we should also exhibit restraint in their use.

SUMMARY

Luxury is a personal, emotional experience. It may be represented by a service, product, or experience, but it is the feeling of pleasure, the enjoyment of something refined, rare, and of the highest quality.

For The Rich Minimalist, it is best to enjoy One Well-Chosen Luxury. It may be an elegant, discreet, timeless wristwatch. It may be a certain blends of artisan tea. It may be a spa day at a resort.

Whatever your Luxury is, it is, by definition, limited in quantity and of the highest quality. It is the thing that makes you feel like the work, discipline, and sacrifice are worth it. You should be able to enjoy your One Well-Chosen Luxury in private. It is not for display. It is not to be bragged about. It is for personal pleasure.

Exercise: Sit down with a pen and paper. Make a list of the Luxuries that you enjoy or would like to enjoy. You may have an inventory of five or ten products, services, or experiences. Once you have the list, put them in order of preference. Now, look at the top Luxury on your list. Are you willing to sacrifice all the other Luxuries to enjoy that One Well-Chosen Luxury? That's the test.

Also, remember that this One Well-Chosen Luxury should mesh with the Ten Rich Minimalist Luxuries that we discussed in this chapter. It doesn't have to come after all of these intangible Luxuries, but it must be in harmony with them, and not enjoyed at the expense of the others.

The Importance of Purpose

His mind on other things, a greedy and selfish man hurried along a crowded city sidewalk and stepped into the street where he was immediately hit and killed by a speeding truck.

A moment later, he awoke. Blinking his eyes, he found himself clad in a silk robe, sitting upon a lush velvet sofa, in a glistening marble palace, surrounded by fragrant flowers, with birds cheerily chirping and a cool breeze gently blowing.

A uniformed butler approached him.

"Welcome, sir. What may I get you?"

"What do you mean?" replied the confused man.

"I am here to bring you anything you want. Just tell me what it is," explained the butler.

"Oh," said the man, thinking. "I'd like some champagne and strawberries," he said after a moment, testing the waters of this new realm.

"Excellent choice, sir."

The butler quickly departed and soon returned with a chilled bottle of champagne and a sterling silver bowl of strawberries.

The man sipped the champagne and ate the strawberries, and both were delicious, the best he'd ever tasted. Looking around at his beautiful surroundings, he grew quite pleased with himself and even chuckled at his apparent good fortune.

After awhile, the butler returned. "Is there something else I can bring you, sir?"

"I'm feeling a little chilly," said the man, now more comfortable making requests. "Could I get something to put around my shoulders?"

"Of course, sir."

And soon the butler returned with a crimson cashmere blanket. It was the most exquisite fabric, so very light and soft and warm.

As he was greedy and selfish, the man nestled into the blanket and began to quickly consider the next thing he might want for himself.

The butler soon returned. "Is there something else I can bring you, sir?"

"You know, I think I'd like to go for a walk, get some exercise, perhaps read a book."

"I'm sorry, sir. That is not possible."

"What do you mean?" replied the confused, annoyed, and slightly indignant man.

"You can have anything you want," said the butler matter-of-factly, "but you are not permitted to do anything."

"That doesn't sound right. That doesn't sound like paradise!"

"Sir," responded the butler, arching an eyebrow, "where do you think you are?"

Jean-Paul Sartre, the French philosopher, once quipped, "Hell is other people." He might have been joking. A more accurate statement would be, "Hell is having nothing to do."

With that truth in mind, here are the most important concepts for you to remember as you embrace The Rich Minimalist way of life:

In order to comfortably live with fewer material possessions, reach your full potential, be happy, and become rich, you must have a purpose in life. The challenge is to discover and define that purpose.

You should be able to state your purpose in one simple sentence or phrase.

Like your One Well-Chosen Luxury, this is your One Big Thing in Life.

It is helpful to keep your purpose in the forefront of your mind, writing it down, and repeating it to yourself often.

Once you know what your purpose is, you can then determine the direction you need to move in, define the steps you need to take in order to fulfill your purpose, and recognize the benchmarks that can measure your progress along the way.

Your purpose fuels your work, most often expressed in your occupation or profession.

If your daily work is done on purpose, that is, if it is aligned with your talents and overall aim in life, then it is more likely to be meaningful and rewarding, both emotionally and financially.

If other choices—your lifestyle and relationships—also align with your purpose, you live in harmony and are more likely to need less, accumulate more wealth, and be happy.

The larger and nobler the purpose, the richer and more fulfilling the life.

However, even a narrower or more limited purpose can bring contentment. For example, one person may want to be President of the United States so that she can help her fellow man. Another person may want to put his only child through college in order to give her more opportunities and options in life.

One person's purpose is never more valid or more important than another person's purpose.

Your purpose is your purpose. It doesn't matter what other people think of it.

Your purpose should be constructive, life-affirming, and achievable as a result of your actions and choices. It should not be a contingent upon the expectations or obligations you place on others.

Your purpose should challenge you to be and do your best.

The accomplishment of your purpose should be good for you, those you care about, and the world.

Living a purpose-driven life will reframe your idea of 'success'. It will change your definition of the word.

Living 'on purpose' will change your priorities, away from buying and having, toward being and doing.

This in turn will increase your productivity.

This in turn will increase your profitability.

This in turn will increase your wealth, making you rich.

I placed this chapter near the end of the book because it is the most important concept for you to understand and embrace.

A Final Thought

Now that you realize you can't take it with you, what are you going to leave behind?

Minimalism has been the lifestyle of the wise for a very long time, even if it was not known by that name.

Today, we face challenging economic times around the world and a nagging sense of discontent within ourselves. We often find life as a 'continuous consumer' financially unsustainable and emotionally unfulfilling. We want to change.

Becoming a Rich Minimalist is a viable option for those who wish to improve their quality of life, accelerate the speed at which they achieve financial independence, and enjoy the true luxuries that life has to offer.

As our planet and our society pay the price for centuries of consumerism, the way forward is clear. The Rich Minimalist philosophy and practice is the future.

Embrace it.

Master it.

Enjoy it.

And prosper.

Rich Minimalist Meditations

Discover the One Big Thing for your life. Commit to it.

Curate your One Well-Chosen Luxury. Revel in it.

Guard your thoughts. Watch your words. Confront your fears. Live your dreams.

It's better for people to see that you've changed, rather than to hear you talk about everything you're going to change.

Prayer is asking. Meditation is listening.

Yoga, light weights, stationary bike, daily.

Walk, bike, public transportation, car, in that order.

Prevention first, cure second.

Vegetarian or vegan diet. For your health. For your planet.

Better alone than in a toxic relationship.

And you are never truly alone.

Social media for business. Privacy for life.

Minimalism requires maintenance.

Fewer things, more life. Fewer things, more money.

Quality over quantity.

Fewer opinions. More information.

Not everyone is you.

Quick to help, slow to judge.

Less television. More books.

Less gossip. More conversation.

More charity, less consumption. Less consumption, more independence. More independence, more opportunity. More opportunity, more wealth. More wealth, and again, more charity.

Confidence. An essential element on the road to success. Absolute certainty. A common sentiment on the road to disaster.

Be silent in the face of adversity. Be vocal in the face of injustice.

Retire your idols. Be your own hero.

Let work be your worship. Let passion be your guide.

Thought/word/deed. All in line. All the time.

Let self-respect be your most prized possession. Sacrifice it for nothing.

ABOUT THE AUTHOR

Byron Tully is best known as the author of *The Old Money Book – How To LIve Better While Spending Less – Secrets of America's Upper Class*. Published in 2014, the book has become an instant classic. Now available in numerous languages, it continues to entertain, inform, and inspire readers around the world.

Byron is also the author of other Old Money titles, as well as nonfiction titles focused on personal finance. For more than a decade, he has curated The Old Money Book blog (www.theoldmoneybook.com) where he posts on a wide range of subjects.

He lives with his wife in Paris.

Also by Byron Tully

How To Be a Rich Man . . . or Woman!
Everyone's Step-by-Step Guide to Creating Wealth

Old Money, New Woman:
How to Manage Your Money and Your Life

The Hindu Way To Wealth:
My Private Conversations with
One of India's Richest Men

The Old Money Guide To Marriage:
Getting It Right and Making It Last

The Old Money Book:
How to Live Better While Spending Less—
Secrets of America's Upper Class